Praise for *Models of Jesus*

"Father O'Grady has attempted a courageous venture: to synthesize much technical language in such a sensitive area . . . He deserves praise for his work and I'm sure that his book will be illuminating for many . . . He surely demonstrates the value of pluralism that is part of our contemporary theological scene. And Christians need to understand the strengths and weaknesses in the various ways we can reflect on the mystery of Christ."—*St. Anthony Messenger*

". . . an act of logic and an act of charity that will certainly help us recognize Jesus both in Scripture and in all our brothers and sisters, to realize that we can best choose Christ as our model by actually imitating that model for the sake of humanity."—*B. C. Catholic*

". . . a unique and scholarly volume dealing with the Christological debate which is so prevalent in our day . . . deep and thought provoking."—*The Bookstore Journal*

"Father O'Grady explains each model in detail and analyzes it from the perspective of helping or hindering our understanding of Jesus . . . He reminds us that 'we are involved with the mystery of human life and the mystery of God and surely there can never be an adequate expression of these realities.' A valuable contribution to the often-controversial discussion of Christology today."—*U. S. Catholic*

". . . a clear and sympathetic treatment of Christology . . . this book can be quite valuable as an undergraduate resource for contemporary Christologies or for adult education courses."—*Theological Studies*

MODELS OF JESUS

MODELS OF JESUS

John F. O'Grady

Complete and Unabridged

IMAGE BOOKS

A Division of Doubleday & Company, Inc.
Garden City, New York
1982

Image Book edition published September 1982 by special arrangement with Doubleday & Company, Inc.

Nihil obstat
Myles M. Bourke, S.T.L., S.S.L.
Censor deputatus

Imprimatur
✠ Howard J. Hubbard, D.D.
   Bishop of Albany
   December 8, 1980

Library of Congress Cataloging in Publication Data
O'Grady, John F
   Models of Jesus.
   Includes index.
   1. Jesus Christ—Person and offices.   I.   Title.
[BT202.O34 1982]   232
ISBN: 0-385-17321-0   *AACR2*
Library of Congress Catalog Card Number: 82-45076

For happy memories.

To the memory of
Nora Gallagher O'Grady
1900–1977

CONTENTS

PREFACE 11

1. THE PRESENT STATE OF CHRISTOLOGY 15

2. JESUS AS THE INCARNATION
   OF THE SECOND PERSON
   OF THE BLESSED TRINITY 41

3. THE MYTHOLOGICAL CHRIST 67

4. JESUS THE ETHICAL LIBERATOR 87

5. THE HUMAN FACE OF GOD 111

6. THE MAN FOR OTHERS 139

7. JESUS, PERSONAL SAVIOR 159

8. THE SEARCH FOR A BIBLICAL
   CHRISTOLOGY 177

9. EVALUATING THE MODELS 195

INDEX 209

PREFACE

THE STUDY OF Jesus of Nazareth has always intrigued me. Like most Christians, I have experienced a spiritual odyssey, having struggled with the meaning of Jesus in a personal way for several years. No doubt, believers experience different stages in their acceptance of the Lord and with those stages come new insights and new understanding.

To someone who has grown up accepting Jesus as the Word of God Incarnate, it might appear difficult to change models, although, for me, it happened long before the model change was formulated or even adverted to.

Growth in faith suggests subtle changes which often take place without much awareness. Then, suddenly, a person finds himself or herself far removed from the starting point.

This book is written to give some direction, some clarification and even to provoke some new movements in faith. I hope to open up some of the various approaches to Jesus that are not only possible, but actual, in the Church today.

The original idea for this book came from a casual remark by the Rev. Richard McBrien of the University of Notre Dame. We had discussed Christology and then began to explore some models of Jesus. With that as a beginning, the book gradually took shape in my mind.

I have learned from experience that most of my good ideas come from interaction with others. In writing this book, I am particularly indebted to several friends who gave not only their ideas, but cogent suggestions for approach, for methodology and for style. I am particularly indebted to Dr. Anne Minton and the Rev. Robert McNamara, both colleagues at St. Bernard's Seminary in Rochester. They read the entire manuscript and were most helpful.

The Rev. Dr. Joseph P. McClain, C.M., was the first to introduce me to Christology as a young student of theology. I continue to learn from him and am conscious of my debt to him for his suggested improvements of Chapter 2. Dr. George S. Worgul of Duquesne University was also helpful with suggestions for revising Chapter 5. The Rev. Dr. Theodore Weeden, Sr., also a colleague in Rochester, offered valuable suggestions concerning New Testament Christology and the theology of R. Bultmann. Without the help of these friends, not only would the thought be of less value, but the work itself would be less adequate in relating the meaning of the models of Jesus.

It is my hope that this book will continue the work of evangelization, which is the heart of the mission of Jesus.

Monterey, Mass. *January, 1980*

MODELS OF JESUS

1

THE PRESENT STATE
OF CHRISTOLOGY

DISCUSSIONS ABOUT the Old Testament and its meaning cause little reaction among Christians. Unfortunately, for many Christians what happened to the Jews and the record of their relationship with God are not as important as what happened to Jesus. This attitude, especially in Roman Catholic circles, has created a situation that encouraged the scientific study of the Old Testament but remained wary of a similar approach to the New Testament.

In 1943 Pius XII published his encyclical *Divino Afflante Spiritu*[1] and for the first time Roman Catholic scholars were encouraged to use a scientific method in the study of the Bible. The green light was given, however, mainly for the Old Testament, not for the New. It was not until the *Declaration on the Truth of the Gospels*[2] in 1964 that Roman Catholic scholars could feel free to use the methods of contemporary scholarship in regard to the New Testament. Since that time we have seen an interest in biblical studies that has profoundly altered the understanding of Christianity and has implications for the Church of the next century.

The results of this scholarship have clearly affected the understanding of Jesus and, as a result of the new atmosphere in the Church after the Second Vatican Council, the findings have not been limited to obscure journals. Most Christians are aware of what theologians are saying about Jesus even if sometimes they are confused by the publicity involved. Accordingly, the time has come to state clearly the present state of Christology, to examine the various approaches that have characterized theology over the centuries, and to examine certain of the ideas that are prevalent today.

Recently, theologians have been studying the Church, seeking to understand how personal images of the Church might influence attitudes and behavior.[3] The result has been a healthier attitude toward the divergent opinions that can exist within the Church without doing harm to its basic meaning. The same should be true with regard to Jesus.

At the outset, however, we can expect a certain resistance. When a scientific methodology is applied to the New Testament, and to Jesus, more traditional-minded individuals are apt to react negatively. The same might be true if we begin to entertain the thought that divergent views on Christology can well be admitted within the Church.

In 1972 the Congregation for the Defense of the Faith published a declaration entitled "Safeguarding Basic Christian Beliefs."[4] In this document the Congregation saw the need to reiterate certain traditional Roman Catholic teachings with regard to Jesus and the Trinity. There was concern that some of the teachings of the Christian faith were being undermined by certain contemporary theologians and thus the Church would have to react to affirm the traditional approach to Christology and to the Trinity. Much of the concern seems to have arisen because of the new terminology in Christology as well as the efforts to encounter again what has been the Christian heritage on Jesus. The effort to reexamine such teachings as the meaning of preexistence, the one divine person, and the presence of the human person in Jesus, are presented in the declaration as contrary to true belief in Christ.[5]

After the declaration was published, Pope Paul VI called attention to the statement in his usual Sunday audience and explained why such a statement was necessary. He said that recently the teachings on Jesus had not been properly interpreted.[6] The Pope continued that such statements had spread even among "us believers." Therefore, the Congregation responded. The conclusion of the declaration, however, should not be overlooked. In spite of their anxiety, the authors of the statement admit the need for updating traditional dogmatic formulations.[7] More recently, the decision by the Congregation for the Defense of the Faith to investigate and censure certain European theologians may be read as continual signs of anxiety with regard to the contemporary research on the meaning of Jesus. In spite of the anxiety, the research continues.

If theology is faith seeking understanding, then there will be a continual growth in an appreciation of Jesus and his gospel. No one generation can claim to speak the last word or disclose the final expression. Each generation must examine the insights of the past in order to offer new generations of believers an understanding of Jesus that will be intelligible to the contemporary spirit. Often enough, in the contemporary research on Jesus, we are not concerned with faith as much as past interpretations of faith. For a theologian to reexamine some of the fundamental tenets of Christian belief does not imply a doubt of those beliefs. With the passage of time, words change in meaning—or at least in nuance. To be faithful to its task, theology will always demand a study of what words have meant in the past and what they might mean today. The theologian is conscious of our common Christian heritage, but also of the responsibility to reinterpret that heritage.

If Christian theology in general continually needs updating, this is certainly true of the heart of Christian theology, the study of Jesus. When the Church encouraged the scientific investigation of the New Testament, it was also commending the careful methodological approach to Jesus as advocated by most contemporary theologians.

In a speech prior to the Second Vatican Council, Pope John XXIII was most careful to distinguish the content of faith from its expression:

> *The deposit of faith is one thing; the way that it is presented is another. For the truths preserved in our sacred doctrine can retain the same substance under different forms of expression.*[8]

The problem arises when theologians actually try to fulfill their function in the Church and begin to use new terminology which is either not understood by the official Church or does not meet with approval among the majority of believers. The problem is compounded when popular newsmagazines take learned articles and digest them into one-page religion sections with startling headlines announcing that theologians question the divinity of Jesus.

Scholastic philosophers often remarked that whatever is perceived is perceived according to the mode of the perceiver. We might paraphrase this axiom in contemporary language and state: "People hear what they want to hear." Surely that is true with regard to the present state of Christology.

For those who have been nurtured on a "docetic" or a totally spiritual or divine Christ, anything that seems to emphasize the humanity of Jesus will be suspect. For someone who has viewed Christ as the suffering servant going to his death meek and humble, any effort to make him a social reformer is simply out of order and in contradiction to the gospel. For anyone who has regarded Jesus as the all-knowing God in human form, certain of the attitudes of Jesus in the gospels need to be explained or nuanced.[9] How could he ask questions when he knew everything? The only explanation would be that Jesus, like Socrates, questions as a pedagogical technique.

Someone who sees Jesus as a good man—as an individual who could identify with the human condition and could rise above that condition—would consider any attempt to deny that he lived a human life (by making him out to be God) as tantamount to the destruction of the meaning of Jesus.[10] Anyone who sees the need to reform the social order on the basis of the gospel will not be content to adhere in belief to a God-man who is content to live under any social system, even an unjust one.[11]

In reality we come face to face with the question of the many images of Jesus. It is easy to refer to the question of Jesus himself in the gospels: "Who do you say that I am?" (Mark 8:27) and think that all will give the same answer. In the history of Christianity, however, such agreement is nonexistent. There are often as many answers as people who choose to respond, and even those who refuse to respond often have their unspoken answer. People still hear what they want to hear. If a person adheres in faith to a Jesus who is the Second Person of the Blessed Trinity, then everything about Jesus is judged in that light. If someone else sees only the good man who suffered and died unjustly, no amount of rhetoric will persuade that person otherwise.

Recently the Roman Catholic tradition has been exposed to the thought that there are many models of the Church. Some see the Church as a visible institution, others as a mystical communion, as a sacrament, as a herald or as a servant. Each model offers some insight into the meaning of the Church; each offers some understanding—but if viewed exclusively, each model breaks down and fails in its ability to represent the true reality in any complete or final fashion.

Some of the people who read Dulles' book *Models of the Church* or McBrien's *The Remaking of the Church* clearly can identify with one or the other of the models. This colors not only their reaction to opinions about the Church, but also their actions as members of the Church. The Scholastics also had an axiom: Action follows being. What a person is will determine the activity. If a person accepts the institutional model as the only model or as the primary model, then a person's activity will follow suit. Whatever will lessen the institutional aspect in any way must be countered. If a person's primary model is the Church as sacrament or as servant, then there is often little interest in what we would call the visible structure of the Church and little regard for such things as hierarchy, official teachings, etc.[12]

Gradually the notion that the use of models provides a good approach seems to have penetrated within the body of the Church, affecting hierarchy and laity alike. Individuals can now acknowledge their opinions of the Church and not feel afraid of professing one model, since they know that it is only one of several and should not be accepted as the exclusive model without some consideration of other opinions. Even when the choice of a primary model is made, believers are aware that complementary or even opposing opinions have a right to be heard.

If we have reached the point in the history of Christianity when it is acceptable to maintain different models of the Church without detriment to the unity of belief, is it not time to accept a similar position with regard to Jesus? At first such a proposal may well lead to the following reaction: If we allow such a development, we will sacrifice the clarity that has been part of the Christian tradition for centuries. There should not be many models of Jesus, but only one model, which has been expressed in the official teaching of the Church in the course of its development—in particular, through the ecumenical councils.

No doubt, we did have clarity in the past with regard to Christology. The Council of Chalcedon made its dec-

laration and purported to have settled the question for
all time:

> . . . *one the same Christ, the Son, the Lord, only
> begotten, in two natures unconfused, unchangeable,
> undivided, inseparable. The difference of natures will
> never be abolished by their being united but rather
> the properties of each remain unimpaired, both com-
> ing together in one person and substance, not parted
> or divided among two persons but in one and the
> same only begotten Son, the divine Word, the Lord
> Jesus.*[13]

On the fifteen-hundredth anniversary of the Council,
a group of German scholars published a series of articles on Chalcedon. Karl Rahner's contribution was entitled "Chalcedon, Beginning or End?"[14] For this re-
nowned theologian, the Council of Chalcedon did not
represent the end of theological speculation, nor the end
of the debate within the Christian community as to the
meaning of Jesus, but a beginning—a starting point that
would allow further development and refinement, and
continual updating. The clarity of the conciliar definition has been paid for with the loss of continual rethinking that is so essential if Christianity is to make
sense of the central mystery of the faith to all generations.

Fortunately, while the councils have made efforts to
clarify and control, they have also consistently pointed
out that in the end we are dealing with mystery. The
term "mystery" has been used in many ways in the
Bible as well as in the history of theology.[15] Accordingly, it is useful to recall that history provides a starting point for the continual quest that challenges the
theologian.

In Scripture the word "mystery" does not mean
something we can never know, but rather the plan of
God that brings salvation to all through the coming of
Jesus of Nazareth. In Jesus "the manifold wisdom of

God is made known" (Eph. 3:8); "in him dwells the fullness of divinity" (Col. 3:9). In him the mystery that God has preserved for all times has been revealed: "To unite all things in him, things in heaven and things on earth" (Eph. 1:10).

This great mystery is not so much of God in himself, nor even of Jesus in himself, but rather of the relationship between God and his creation, a plan to unite all things in heaven and on earth, a destiny for all creatures to share in the unity of God and realize the perfection that is inherent in creation.

Paul can write in Romans:

> We know that the whole of creation has been groaning in travail, together until now and not only the creation but we ourselves who have the first fruits of the Spirit groan inwardly as we await for adoption as sons the redemption of our bodies. (Rom. 8:22–23)

God the Father has involved himself in his creation through Jesus and his plan is to accomplish the unity of all reality through his Christ.

If in the course of centuries people of faith have sought to understand this mystery, what actually happened was that they themselves were brought into a greater awareness of the meaning of God and his plan of salvation. No one person could ever reach the point of a full understanding or a complete appreciation of this mystery. Even the collective experience of the Church has not exhausted the reality that was the meaning of Jesus and his salvation. If at the outset of this work I choose to speak of mystery, then, it is because I am aware that any theologian faces inexhaustible intelligibility as he or she tries to encounter in a personal way the meaning of Jesus the Christ.[16] We are faced with a richness that cannot be captured in any one model nor in any one period of time, nor by any one individual.

Jesus can be known and experienced more fully and immediately than he can be explained and expressed.

There is a kind of connaturality between believer and the believed. In the presence of such an intimate relationship all attempts at analysis, at moving from the nonconceptual to the conceptual, are doomed to frustration. We are too involved with the mystery of Jesus to ever objectify its meaning. A certain intersubjectivity, which is the basis of faith in the first place, precludes a complete categorical expression.

The Church Fathers of the Second Vatican Council were well aware of the continual need to grow in understanding of this mystery when they related the mystery of Jesus to that of the Church and saw all as part of the divine plan to unite all things in Jesus.[17] The concept of mystery not only places certain limitations on the content of this study, it also affects methodology. We cannot extrapolate from clear, unequivocal concepts or definitions. We cannot simply take the pronouncement of a council and maintain that these concepts are the final and irrevocable approach to the understanding of Jesus. Neither can we simply apply the concepts we abstract from our personal experience to the mystery of God nor to the mystery of Jesus. We may know something of the meaning of personhood, since we have the experience of being persons, but to presume to extend this interpretation to the mystery of God should cause us to hesitate. We may also have some concepts of the meaning of being human—not just through personal experience, but also by means of the collectivity; but to delineate what it means to be divine should stop us in our tracks. Our learned concepts are not directly applicable to the mystery that is the plan of God to unite all things in himself. As a result, some people have given up the quest.

We can become quietists if we so choose and ignore the theological endeavor. Since we will never have all the answers and since even what approximates an answer is provisional, why should the Christian engage in any theological speculation?

The easiest response to this question is to acknowledge that evidently God has chosen to communicate to us through Jesus and so there must be some value for us in struggling with the interaction of the divine and human, even if the final outcome is in shadow. It is furthermore a denial of the gifts of the human spirit to retreat and remain silent about the meaning of God in Jesus.

Throughout the history of Christianity we come face to face with various images of Jesus. Nowhere is this more evident than in various portrayals of Jesus in Christian art. If one were to do a comparative study through the ages, one would find that there is a clear relationship between popular piety (another form of images) and the artistic depictions of the Lord. The statue of Jesus at the portal of the thirteenth-century Cathedral of Chartres is strong and commanding. He holds a book. The statue is entitled "The Teaching Lord." The artist has a clear image of Jesus as one who commands respect and teaches with authority. At the same time, the facial expression is kind and gentle. Jesus' eyes are soft and warm, his lips curved slightly in a smile. Compare this image from the thirteenth century with the figure on many of the holy cards of the twentieth century associated with devotion to the Sacred Heart. Often the features are weak and ethereal; there is little power, and at times there is even a sadness that does not inspire.

The history of theology also has its images—what we call models, or symbols, or paradigms. They have a long history in the learned traditions of Christianity as well as in the ordinary heritage of believers. We have noted already how such models have returned on the theological scene. The basis for such diverse images is to be found in the New Testament itself.

In the gospels and the other writings of the early Church we find myriad images of Jesus which formed various foundations for speculation about his meaning.

Jesus is the lamb of God, the Word, the prophet, the messiah, the almighty Lord of heaven and earth; he is the servant who assumes humble tasks and who suffers unjustly. Jesus is the teacher who teaches with power; he is the miracle worker who performs prodigies as the healer. Jesus is also the vine, the shepherd, the door, the gate, the light. Each of these images of Jesus captures some aspect of his person. No one image can be thought to be the exclusive portrayal of the meaning of the Lord, but each one does contribute to an overall picture. The Bible is filled with many images, since it is the record of the experience of the early Church, which held in its collective consciousness many faces of Jesus.

When we study the history of Christology we also are aware of the use of images. For some early believers he was a divine man (*theios aner*). Some heretics saw him as a gnostic redeemer come to gather together the various sparks of light that had been scattered in the human race. Later theology would see him as the Second Person of the Blessed Trinity. Certain contemporary theologians see him as the man for others; still others regard Jesus as the great liberator.

All of the above images, whether from the New Testament, from the history of theology, from Christian art or common piety, reveal psychological and existential aspects of people who believe in Jesus. They are signs and they are symbols. They reach down into the very depth of the reality of Jesus and bring up some aspect of his person that appeals to the human psyche. How much of the reality is actually made present depends upon the particular choice of image or symbol. Some symbols communicate through evoking a response. The face of Jesus from Chartres, for example, evokes a sense of trust and confidence. Other images appeal more to the conceptual side of human nature. Symbols of Jesus can transform a person's attitude toward life; they can integrate perceptions, change value systems, reorient loyalties and create a sense of commitment and attachment far stronger than abstract concepts. Good symbols have more than just an intellectual appeal and more than just an aesthetic appeal. They are involved with the whole person—with all of the facets that create a human being in concrete human existence. If they are able to make the reality known, it is more than an academic exercise. The symbol actually contains the reality it expresses[18] and thus can engage the person and focus the human experience in a definite way.

Any group of people that hopes to remain bound together in some sense of unity will depend on symbols to help them accomplish that task. We are familiar from the history of Christianity with the symbol of the fish used by early believers for Jesus. The five Greek letters for fish were an acronym for Jesus Christ, Son of God, Savior. From recent secular history we know of the use of the swastika, which helped unite people in a fanatic commitment to a dictator; we are also aware of the symbol for peace that was used extensively throughout the Sixties and Seventies. The clenched fist is often used by those who claim power even if they do not experience that power. The Olympic torch is a symbol known throughout the world. A good symbol can arouse many feelings: courage, peace, authority, hatred and love.

When we examine the images of Jesus they suggest attitudes, feelings, courses of action and devotion. They help to unite people together into a common bond of affection and commitment. But always, as images, they are incomplete and should not be seen as perfect in themselves. They are expressions of the reality toward which they can lead, but for which they cannot substitute.[19]

For an image to gain acceptance, it must conform to the experience of people of faith. At the same time, the images help to shape that faith. The community must learn from the experience of its individual members with regard to images and at the same time must help inspire images for their edification. To be effective, the image or symbol must be deeply rooted in the experience of the community of believers. The Church is not dependent upon an image that is short-lived or based upon the experience of a limited few or of a particular period in the history of faith. The true symbols will eventually rise to the surface, even if there is a period of confusion and a multiplicity of inadequate and unworthy images. It is essential to recall the limited value of even the best of images. They are helpful, but should not be perceived as absolutes.

In our present period of Church history we seem to be experiencing a crisis of images. This is not limited to the religious sphere, for our previous relatively stable culture suddenly seems no longer firmly established. The rapid change in the Western arena has caused a breakdown in some of the most common symbols and images of human life. Kings rise and fall; presidents who are supposed to epitomize the best of American traditions misuse power and become symbols of the worst. The stability of great universities as symbols of longevity and learning and integrity is compromised by involvement with government or business control; schools are torn in many directions, with student and faculty crises. Banks, considered to be the foundation of economic stability, actually close their doors. If the symbols that help to unite disparate elements of society appear to be crumbling, it is not surprising that people are afraid and confused.

With regard to the Church, perhaps it is not so much a crisis of faith that we face, but a crisis of images. The Roman Catholic Church used to convey stability; the rock of Peter was truly a rock. Religious men and women portrayed a sense of commitment and symbolized this commitment in action and even in dress—but now the images have been altered and people feel insecure.

The crisis is not, of course, just limited to the understanding of the Church. The entire Christian message is based upon images. These images, however, are often taken from pastoral scenes and never from the twentieth-century technological society. Most people have little contact with lambs and shepherds, or even with vines and grapes. Servants, where they exist, are not in the same social category as in the time of Jesus.

There is a need to examine the images of the past and to supplement these images with others that are more in conformity with the faith community that has been reforming itself for the past two hundred years. The development of the new images will continue wherever the faith is vibrant. A problem we face today, however, is that, although our Church has already decided to make many changes in its outward appearance, in consonance with changes that have taken place in our secular culture, the images of Jesus have not kept pace with the experience of the larger community. Our language has become impoverished with regard to religious imagery because there seems to be so little in our experience that bears the stamp of the numinous.

In spite of this, we do have examples of creative theological thinking. J.A.T. Robinson derived his image of Jesus as the human face of God[20] from the theology of the later Barth;[21] Dietrich Bonhoeffer was the first to speak of Jesus as the Man for Others.[22] Edward Schillebeeckx coined the phrase "Jesus as the sacrament of encounter" to explain his sacramental theology.[23] Karl Rahner sees Jesus in relationship to the evolution of man and thus the image is that of a perfected human person.[24] For any of the above images to catch on, there is need of the *kairos*, the right time. The religious community must be psychologically set for the image. With Tillich, we are aware that images are not created or destroyed by human effort; they are born or they die. They often acquire a mysterious power that seems beyond man's control or even beyond his comprehension.[25]

We are surely aware of the importance of images in

human life and of how essential they are for the life of the believer. We live and die with images and by images. In our efforts to communicate our faith, we must constantly try to find new images that can convey something of that faith. When St. Patrick stumbled upon the shamrock as the image of the Trinity, he was being faithful to the human need to express concretely an abstract notion. Recently an East Coast diocese chose to use a logo of people gathered together in a tight circle to symbolize a program of reconciliation inaugurated by the bishop. This logo was spread throughout the diocese and helped to raise people's awareness of the program.[26]

Theology also depends upon images and symbols, as we have already noted. For a true theology, however, along with the symbol comes analysis. We cannot settle for the shamrock for the symbol of the Trinity without analysis. What meets the needs on the level of catechetics does not always reach the level of theology. Nor must the theologian limit his interest to those images that are current. We can study the symbols of the past, even if they have lost some of their power, to uncover some new vitalization that can be used today. It is also possible to examine some of the current symbols and see what value they are actually conveying. The theologian is not always the preacher, and so the person who tries to proclaim Jesus to the ordinary believer must be careful to choose images that convey some sense of understanding, just as the theologian must be aware of what is actually being preached. The theologian always seeks to study and analyze symbols. If the time is a *kairos*, the person devoted to the study of Jesus may actually help to form a symbol that is acceptable to the collective spirit of the faith community.

When a theologian seeks to use a particular image in theology, he is primarily interested in gaining some insight into the understanding of faith. The theologian is aware of the usefulness of the images, but also aware of limitations. No symbol contains the fullness of the reality, and thus no one particular image can be erected into an absolute, nor can it ever be construed as a substitute for the reality itself. The good theologian will use images reflectively and with sobriety. As someone dedicated to the careful study of the faith, the theologian is anxious to evaluate critically the images of the past as well as the images of the present, in an effort to distinguish what is a valid expression of some aspect of the mystery of faith from what is judged as inadequate, invalid or even prejudicial to faith.

When an image is used theologically, reflectively and critically to deepen one's theoretical understanding of a reality, it becomes what is called a model. Some models are also images; that is, they can be imagined easily. Other models are more abstract. With regard to Jesus, we can model him as a shepherd, or as a preacher or a prophet. To model him as the Second Person of the Blessed Trinity or the Word of God, however, does not connote the idea of an image, since the ideas are more abstract.

The physical sciences and the social sciences have used models extensively in the past. Only recently have models been used in theology. We have already noted the choice of the title of the book by Avery Dulles on the Church. I. T. Ramsey also demonstrates how the use of models can be helpful in theology.[27] There are obvious similarities and differences between the way the various sciences use models and the way theology uses them. In science the use of models is effective if the model allows for deductions as well as verification: "In any scientific understanding a model is better, the more prolific it is in generating deductions which are then open to experimental verification and falsification."[28] A model that fails to respond to some of the questions to be answered is by that fact limited in its usefulness. A model that does not allow for experimentation is also of limited value, since the researcher cannot verify the truth purported to be represented.

With certain restrictions, we can apply these notions to theology, even though they have been developed primarily in other fields. E. Cousins explains clearly the use of models in theology:

> *Theology is concerned with the ultimate level of religious mystery which is even less accessible than the mystery of the physical universe. Hence our religious language and symbols should be looked upon as models because even more than the concepts of science, they only approximate the object they are reflecting.*[29]

Previously we have noted the necessity of avoiding making the symbol an absolute. Cousins is convinced that the use of a model prevents this possibility:

> *to use the concept of model in theology, then, breaks the illusion that we are actually encompassing the infinite within our finite structures and language. It prevents concepts and symbols from becoming idols and opens theology to variety and development just as the model method has done for science. Yet there is a danger that it will not go far enough for it may not take sufficiently into account the level of religious experience.*[30]

The last comment of Cousins is telling. There are certain disadvantages in using a methodology from the physical sciences. Religious experience is more than intellectual; it involves the entire person. We cannot compare our religious faith with our analysis of the universe in any complete fashion. Analysis can be used, but in all analogies the differences predominate. In faith we come face to face with more than can be contained in any model. Recognizing this deficiency, however, we can also see that models can help the theologian not only in efforts to explain faith, but in exploring faith.

On the level of explanation, models tend to synthesize what we have already experienced or have come to believe in our faith experience. Just as a good scientific model will synthesize and respond to many facets and problems and questions, so the theological model will synthesize the biblical experience as well as the experience of centuries of lived faith in the history of Christianity.

The gospel models of Jesus as a shepherd, or the lamb of God, or one of the prophets convey certain aspects of the meaning of Jesus, and the Church has accepted them. He is the one who provides for and protects; he is the one who offers himself without hesitation to God his Father; he is the one who fulfills the aspirations of the Old Testament and points out the religious dimension present or absent in human life. Each model points out one specific aspect of Jesus and his ministry, but each has its obvious limits. No model above takes into account the specific relationship between Jesus and God his Father. Nor do they deal with an appreciation of Jesus as one like his brethren "in all things but sin" (Heb. 4:15). Thus other models must be used to supplement these models taken from Scripture. In the history of theology, we know that Jesus has been called the Second Person of the Blessed Trinity, the man for others, the sacrament of God, and the human face of God.

In the use of models, we should note that the more applications the models have, the better they suggest a true isomorphism between the reality of Jesus and the image that is used to convey something of that reality. No complete harmony is possible, since the symbol is forever limited in expressing the reality it contains.

With regard to the exploratory use of models, we are involved with the specific theological task of breaking new ground and offering a means for the theologian to fulfill his task as one who is seeking understanding. Such a responsibility is demanding and involves many pitfalls. Somehow the theologian must steer a course between the Scylla of exploration for its own sake and the Charybdis of theological stagnation in long-outdated ideas. Christian theology has a norm in the gospel of Jesus as experienced and expressed in the early Church. Thus in some sense every exploration is a further enunciation of the reality of Jesus always present in his Church. We cannot have any ongoing sense of revelation as the unfolding of the offer of a relationship with God, unless Jesus is with his people now, continuing to offer himself in ways that are meaningful to people of every age. Exploring the present experience of Jesus by the faithful is also part of the theological enterprise. A true development in theology which is not just the unfolding of what was always known does exist, since the present experience of the Church is in a certain sense unique, and that experience itself will bring new insights into the meaning of faith.

The present Pope, John Paul II, has learned from personal experience the role of the Church in a Marxist regime. That in itself gives an understanding of Jesus that would not be possible at any other moment in history. The experience of faith in Latin America or in the emerging nations of Africa and Asia has developed new insights into the meaning of Jesus, and in the Vatican Council it was specifically American experience that gave birth to the decree on religious liberty. In each period of history, theological reflection has nourished insights that grew out of the interchange of human experience and Christian faith. The result has raised the consciousness of the entire Church to appreciate another aspect of the inexhaustible meaning of Jesus of Nazareth.

A further problem in the exploratory use of models in Christology is that of verification. Because we are dealing with the mystery of God and man, we cannot easily deduce nor can we use any empirical tests to see if the model is actually helpful or harmful to Christian faith.

The model of Jesus as ethical liberator, which we shall study in greater detail, causes some to suspect that this must imply the approval of violence and thus cannot be valid. This may not be the case. The model, as we shall see, need not automatically entail the sanctioning of violence, thus contradicting the fundamentally nonviolent stance of Christianity. Clearly, we cannot use empirical tests for verification of this model, since statistics in themselves cannot tell us what is right or wrong in the struggle for justice. The number of people espousing liberation theology in Latin America and in other parts of the world is not a criterion for rightness, nor is the number of people opposed to liberation theology a sign that the model is wrong. Even the presence of some people in the movement who advocate violence does not, of itself, vitiate the value of the model.

Just as the discernment of spirits is necessary in the spiritual life, so too a process of discernment is crucial in the realm of theology. Ignatius Loyola saw the need to seek guidance to discover the significant values in the life of faith. This concept can be applied here as well. K. Rahner faces the question of authority in the Church and speaks of a certain "feel" for the rightness of a position. He speaks of a sense of peace that will be the sign that the person is on the right track:

> That serene, joyous, harmonious lucidity in which there can alone be any hope of finding the correct solution in individually important affairs, may also be the fruit of the spirit.[31]

A corporate discernment of spirits which can be most helpful in coming to some judgment with regard to the use of models for Jesus:

> As this life of Christ is deepened in us by the Holy Spirit there is created in the Christian a "sense of Christ," a taste and instinctual judgment for the things of God, a deeper perception of God's truth, an increased understanding of God's dispositions and

love toward us. This is what Christians must strive to
attain individually and corporately; theologians call it
Christian conaturality. It is like a natural instinct or
intuition but it is not natural, since it results from the
supernatural reality of the divine indwelling and the
impulses of grace.[32]

This feel for what is right or wrong, valid or invalid,
is important in the evaluation of any model. Jesus had
the same idea when he remarked, "By their fruits you
shall know them" (Matt. 7:20). If a model is truly
helpful for faith, the Christian community will recognize it, even though this may take time and involve op-
position. Where the result of the model is anger or dis-
cord or the destruction of individuals in any way, then
we know that the Spirit is not at work. We can evaluate
the models of Jesus by the effect they have on the
Church, the worldwide community of believers who
profess the gospel on which every model must ultimately be based.

Faith is not just a theoretical engagement of the
mind. Faith is lived. Theory and practice are not separate realities. Faith in Jesus exists in people and in history, neither divorced from them nor isolated from
their historical experiences. It is the continual interplay
between the individual believer working out of his or
her own history in conjunction with other believers that
brings faith to birth. When these realities are in balance,
one can confidently judge the validity of a model of
Jesus.

An example from the history of theology should help
to clarify this method of discernment. In medieval times
the model of Jesus as the ultimate ruler of all gave birth
to a sense of judgment and control that produced an
authoritarian Church in the late Middle Ages. If Jesus
controlled all people and if the Church shared in this
power, then the Church had an obligation to rule over
everyone and consequently the Church could forbid
anyone to think differently from the official teaching.

Church leaders also saw themselves empowered to dethrone kings and force infidels to submit to baptism. The model was taken not from the role of Jesus in the gospels, but from the experience of secular, civil authority. Turning Jesus into a secular potentate and then using that model to control the society from which it arose demonstrates just how questionable that particular model was from the outset.

Several times in this work we have remarked that all models used in theology are incomplete. They illuminate certain aspects of Jesus and obscure others. Certainly the model of Jesus as ruler has some foundation in the New Testament. The Father has given to him power and judgment (Jn. 5:22; Matt. 28:18) but this should not be interpreted by our understanding of rulers in secular society. In the study of Jesus we will end up with many models, some of which will have outlived their usefulness based upon the continual growth and perception of the reality of Jesus as still present in his community. Images and models have proliferated in the history of Christianity. With such a multiplicity, often enough the human mind will want to limit the plurality and search for one model that will be the summation or epitome of all.

Is there some model that will unify the data of Scripture and that of the two thousand years of Christian experience? At various times in the history of theology, people have tried to offer such a model. In our terms, that model would then become a paradigm. When a model successfully solves a great many questions and problems and allows for the greatest number of deductions and further invites a variety of personal understandings, then we have the meaning of a paradigm as expressed by T. Kuhn. Paradigms are "concrete puzzle-solutions which, employed as models or examples, can replace explicit rules as a basis for the solution of the remaining puzzles of normal science."[33]

In the past the chief paradigm for Jesus was the Second Person of the Blessed Trinity. This formed the basis for scholastic Christology and has been part of the official teaching of the Church for the past fifteen hundred years. In recent years the Church has chosen to use other models, at least in unofficial documents, but the paradigm has remained the same. The Eternal-Only-Begotten-Son-Second-Person-of-the-Blessed-Trinity is the model that responds to the most questions and problems and allows for the greatest expression of the reality.

The question that I wish to pose is whether this in fact should be the paradigm that the Church uses in the twentieth or twenty-first century? Are we expected to maintain and hold to this paradigm, or can we use it as one model and turn to some other paradigm?

Whatever one's personal position, the transition from one paradigm to another creates problems. Each model brings its strengths and weaknesses. When one model becomes a paradigm, the weaknesses are often forgotten and the strengths are emphasized. When paradigms shift, people who have grown accustomed to the strengths of one and have never been aware of its weaknesses will react sharply against the introduction of a new paradigm. Not only are theologians threatened who have worked out their own positions in terms of the previously reigning paradigm, but ordinary people are affected at the level of their beliefs and practices.

No one should be surprised, then, to find polarization with regard to Jesus and his image in the contemporary Church. Theologians often seem unable to communicate when the official Church falls back on a reaffirmation of more traditional models. In times of controversy the usual tendency is to solidify and reaffirm a previously held tradition. Such is the situation of the Church at the end of the twentieth century; theologians and others must learn not only to live with that fact, but also to gain insights from it. If no one paradigm provides the final answer, then it seems that an acceptance of many models within a dominant paradigm is the only rational and responsible approach. Only further confusion will result from an effort to convert a single model into a final and eschatological one.

Instead of seeking one absolute paradigm, since each one captures only part of the reality, it is healthy for the Christian community to recognize the plurality and celebrate the complementarity of the models. A model may also be erected into a paradigm, but only for a time, and only with the realization that it must accommodate other models.

In the following pages some of the models that have been used with regard to Jesus in the history of Christology will be presented, as well as those models that are currently most popular. To be all-inclusive is impossible, yet I shall try to present these models that have served as paradigms in the past or have the possibility of becoming paradigmatic in the future. I hope to delineate the various approaches to Christology of the past as well as to show the avenues of development in the present. If a theologian adopts a model or a combination of models, by that fact he has committed himself to a particular stance in systematic and practical theology. Action follows being.

I hope to be fair in presenting the models, both their strengths and weaknesses. I will not disguise my position concerning the superiority of one model over the others. This does not deny the contribution of the various models, nor should it prejudice the reader. Rather, taking a position with regard to a possible paradigm represents the responsibility of the theologian. Dante reserved a special place in hell for those who refused to take sides in a controversy. That should never be the position of a theologian.

NOTES

1. See *Rome and the Study of Scripture* (St. Meinrad: Grail, 1962).

.. See *The Pope Speaks*, vol. 10 (1964–65), 86–90. Also ublished in R. Brown, *Crisis Facing the Church* (New York: Paulist, 1975).

.. Avery Dulles, *Models of the Church* (New York: Douleday, 1974). Richard McBrien, *The Remaking of the Church* (New York: Harper & Row, 1973).

. See *The Pope Speaks*, vol. 17 (1972–73), 64–68.

5. *Ibid.*, p. 65.

5. *Ibid.*, p. 69.

7. *Ibid.*, p. 67.

8. *Acta Apostolicae Sedis*, 54 (1962), 792.

9. In Mark 13:32, Jesus remarks that not even the Son knows the day of judgment. Theologians have developed a host of responses in attempting to explain this lack of knowledge, instead of taking the words at their face value.

10. See John F. O'Grady, *Jesus, Lord and Christ* (New York: Paulist, 1972), Chapter 8.

11. See J. Sobrino, *Christology at the Crossroads* (Maryknoll, N.Y.: Orbis, 1978).

12. See Dulles, *Models of the Church*.

13. *Teachings of the Catholic Church*, ed. K. Rahner (Staten Island, N.Y.: Alba House, 1967), p. 154.

14. Karl Rahner, "Chalkedon—Ende oder Anfang," *Das Konzil von Chalkedon*, ed. A. Grillmeier and H. Bacht, vol. 3 (Wurzburg, 1954), 3–49.

15. See Karl Rahner, "The Concept of Mystery in Catholic Theology," *Theological Investigations*, vol. 4 (Baltimore: Helicon, 1966), 36–73. Raymond Brown, "The Semitic Background of the New Testament *Mysterion*," *Biblica*, 39 (1958) 426–48; 40 (1959), 70–87.

16. Rahner, *op. cit.*, 41–43.

17. "Lumen Gentium," *Documents of Vatican II*, ed. Walter Abbott (New York: America Press, 1966).

18. See Karl Rahner, "The Theology of the Symbol," *Theological Investigations*, vol. IV (Baltimore: Helicon, 1966), 221–52.

19. *Ibid.*

20. J.A.T. Robinson, *The Human Face of God* (Philadelphia: Westminster, 1967).

21. Karl Barth, *The Humanity of God* (Richmond, Va.: John Knox, 1960).

22. D. Bonhoeffer, *Letters and Papers from Prison* (New York: Macmillan, 1967).

23. Edward Schillebeeckx, *Christ the Sacrament of Encounter* (New York: Herder and Herder, 1963). See also *Jesus. An Experiment in Christology* (New York: Seabury, 1979).

24. Karl Rahner, *Foundations of Christian Faith* (New York: Seabury, 1978), Chapter VI.

25. Quoted in Dulles, *Models of the Church*, p. 20.

26. During 1979 the Diocese of Albany engaged in a mass-media program directed to a Christian sense of reconciliation. The logo depicting a group of people in a circle was supposed to express the gathering of the people of the Diocese in a spirit of reconciliation. It appeared on bumper stickers, billboards, pins, etc.

27. I. T. Ramsey, *Models and Mysteries* (New York: Oxford, 1964). See also Max Black, *Models and Metaphors* (Ithaca: Cornell University Press, 1962).

28. *Ibid.*, p. 4.

29. E. Cousins, "Models and the Future of Ministry," *Continuum*, 7 (1969), 78–91. John McIntyre, in *The Shape of Christology* (London: SCM Press, 1966) is the first theologian, as far as I can establish, to attempt to use the approach of models in Christology. His particular theological stance differs considerably from mine, but I have profited by his attempts and acknowledge the debt.

30. *Ibid.*

31. Karl Rahner, *The Dynamic Element in the Church* (New York: Herder and Herder, 1964), p. 168.

32. John Powell, *The Mystery of the Church* (Milwaukee: Bruce, 1967), p. 8.

33. T. S. Kuhn, *The Structure of Scientific Revolutions* (Chicago: University Press, 1970), p. 175.

2

JESUS AS THE INCARNATION
OF THE SECOND PERSON
OF THE BLESSED TRINITY

IN THE PREVIOUS chapter several references were made to Jesus as the incarnation of the Second Person of the Blessed Trinity as a paradigm that has influenced Roman Catholic as well as Protestant theology for centuries. Understanding the origin of this paradigm demands a study of the controversies of the first five centuries of the Christian era as well as an appreciation of scholastic theology. While that might be possible in a larger work, here we do better to review the results of these controversies and then strive to uncover the theological development that links the Middle Ages to the twentieth century. This less ambitious approach suits the purpose of this work.

The Council of Chalcedon in 451 is usually presented as the high-water mark for the development of orthodox Christology. At this council such a level of clarity was reached by the Church that it was thought that all subsequent errors in development could be detected by a careful comparison of new ideas with the declaration of the Fathers of Chalcedon. To seek a more profound understanding of Jesus, or a clearer formulation of that understanding, was seen to be not only imprudent but useless. What the official Church had formulated in

Chalcedon after strenuous debate and much controversy between East and West was to become a formula
for all ages.

The previous chapter also made reference to a statement by the Congregation for the Defense of the
Faith.[1] That statement grew out of the conviction that
the Church had already solved the question of the theology of Jesus in previous councils, and in particular at
the Council of Chalcedon. The unanswered question
remains, however: Was Chalcedon the end or the beginning?[2] If it was a plateau to be used as a new starting
point, then continual development is possible. If it was
itself the summit, then there is no need to continue the
search. Before we can develop the model of Jesus as the
incarnation of the Second Person of the Blessed Trinity,
then, we must have some understanding of Chalcedon.

THE COUNCIL OF CHALCEDON

THE ORIGIN of the Council of Chalcedon[3] has roots in
the theological controversy in the Eastern Church on
the precise unity in Jesus and the relationship between
his divinity and humanity. Were there two natures in
Jesus or only one? Did the humanity of Jesus exist first,
to be subsequently assumed into a hypostatic union, or
was the union concomitant with the existence of Jesus?
Is person the same as nature or not? Can you translate
Greek terminology into Latin and vice versa with clarity on both sides? Since the matter was largely centered
in the East, Pope Leo the Great did not wish, at first, to
be involved. Finally, upon the Emperor Theodosius'
convoking a council for August 449 in Ephesus, the
Pope sent legates and presented his famous *Tomus ad
Fulvium*. Leo insisted on the true and integral human
nature of Jesus and in the distinction of natures after
the hypostatic union, which was in one person.[4] He also
described the properties of the human and divine natures, always insisting that it is one and the same person

who possesses both. Those opposed to this formulation entered the council by force, rejected the position of Leo and approved their own. In the history of theology this was called the "Concilium Latronum,"[5] the "council of thieves." Since the matter was not settled at Ephesus, the Council of Chalcedon was called in 451, with representatives from East and West determined to settle the matter.

THE DEFINITION OF CHALCEDON

Following then the Holy Fathers, we all with one voice teach that it should be confessed that Our Lord Jesus Christ is one and the same Son, the same perfect in Godhead, the same perfect in manhood, truly God and truly man, the same [consisting] of a rational soul and body, homoousios [of the same substance] with the Father as to his Godhead, and the same homoousios with us as to his manhood; in all things like unto us, sin only excepted, begotten of the Father before all ages as to his Godhead, and in the last days, the same, for us and for our salvation, of Mary the virgin theotokos as to his manhood.

One and the same Christ, Son, Lord, only begotten, made known in two natures [which exist] without confusion, without change, without division, without separation; the difference in the natures having been in no wise taken away by reason of the union but rather the properties of each being preserved and both concurring into the person [prosopon] and one hypostasis, not parted or divided into two persons [prosopa] but one and the same Son, an only begotten, the divine logos, the Lord Jesus Christ; even as the prophets from of old [have spoken] concerning him, as the Lord Jesus himself has taught us and as the symbol of the faith.[6]

Among other advances, the Council offered clarification on the use of terminology. Previous to this declaration the terminology surrounding the relationship between the humanity and divinity of Jesus was greatly confused. This was particularly evident in the effort to move from Latin to Greek and vice versa. For some theologians nature was the same as *hypostasis*, which was the same as substance, which was the same as *physis*. For others *hypostasis* was the same as person, and nature was the same as *physis*. The Council sought to relate Latin words to Greek words but unfortunately there still remained nuances in meaning that could not be easily translated from one language to another. There was general agreement, but not without some reservations.

There still remained the question of the relationship between the two natures and one person. How was the unity of Jesus to be preserved? The Council stated that there existed two natures, human and divine, in one person, and that there was no confusion of natures. But then how could we understand the unity of Jesus? This involved a further development of trinitarian theology, with the Christological aspect clarified in the sixth century, especially in the works of Leontius, Boethius, Rusticus the Deacon, and Maximus the Confessor. Finally, the matter reached its highest level of development in the scholasticism of the Middle Ages.

Before that, clarification of the subject was reached in the Third Council of Constantinople in 680–81 in which the teachings of Chalcedon were reaffirmed with the additional formulation of the belief that two kinds of will operated in Jesus, the human and the divine.[7] With this formulation the official Church rested its case on the expression of the relationship between the human and the divine in Jesus. Further development would come from the efforts of theologians to interpret and explain this definition. For most of these theologians, Chalcedon was seen as the summit beyond which there was no need for speculation.

THE IMPORTANCE OF CHALCEDON

FINALLY, after more than six hundred years of theological speculation and controversy, the Church expounded a formula of relationship between the humanity and divinity of Jesus. The terminology was not completely clear, since the various factions had different nuances for the same words, but at least there was greater clarification. Now theologians could develop their understanding of Jesus based on the profession of faith as developed by the official Church.

For someone who has read the New Testament, however, these philosophical arguments concerning Jesus can cause much confusion. Have we become so intrigued with formulation that we have lost the reality? For many theologians it is clear that "the simple, original proclamation of Christ, the Revealer, the Bringer of Salvation, the proclamation of Christ the Son of God can be heard in undiminished strength through all the *philosophoumena* of the Fathers,"[8] but for other theologians the development of philosophy has actually obscured this vision. This becomes more evident in the study of the theology of the Middle Ages.

The declaration, as we noted, did not respond to the question of the precise relationship between the two natures and one person in Jesus. In an effort to respond to this question, medieval theologians, followed down into the twentieth century, first studied the Trinity and then situated Christology within their understanding of the former doctrine. They would study the Logos, the Son, in his relationship to Father and Spirit and then deal with the incarnation. Certain theologians have even held the opinion that any one of the divine persons could have become man.[9] The sequence Trinity-creation-fall-incarnation became dominant in theology and lasted for centuries. The great theologians of the Middle Ages also tended to isolate what came to be known as abstract or ontological Christology from concrete or functional Christology. The former deals with the Word of God in relationship to the other persons of the Trinity, particularly the origin of the persons—Father, Son and Spirit—and the precise relationship between the two natures and one person in Jesus. The latter concerns the birth, life, death and resurrection of the Lord and the presence of Jesus as the savior in his Church. Such a division is perfectly consistent with the Thomistic understanding of the object of theology: God in himself, who is attainable by the creature in supernatural immediacy. This has to be treated first before we can deal with the effects of God's action (the incarnation and redemption) on people. This theology derives from an appreciation of the relationship between the Trinity *ad intra* (within itself) and the Trinity *ad extra* (without, in particular, creation, incarnation). All things are thought to originate from God, go forth and then return to the trinitarian fullness. In Christology the Word is seen as that in which all things proceed from and in which all things return to God. If we were to use the terminology discussed in the previous chapter, the model of Christology that resulted from the definition of Chalcedon and the scholastic synthesis is: the Word of God, who is eternal and from whom all things emanate and return. To understand Christology, we must first situate Jesus in the presence of the Blessed Trinity, and then we can come to specific conclusions with regard to the actual redemptive qualities of the life and death of Jesus. After all, the redemption is nothing more than the means by which the eternal Word brings about the restoration of all things in the Trinity from whom all things originated.

The full implications of this model only become clear when we study the various aspects of Christology, namely the motive of the incarnation, the entrance of Jesus into human history, the public ministry of Jesus, his death, resurrection and glorification, and the founding of the Church.

CUR DEUS HOMO? (WHY DID GOD BECOME MAN?)

"WHY DID God become man?" There must have been a purpose, some reason which would have motivated the coming of the Word into human history. The primary area of distinction here is between the Incarnation as prompted by the fall of the human race and the need for its regeneration, and the Incarnation as prompted by the sheer desire of God to share the human condition. Would the Word of God have become human even if humankind had not sinned?

A study of Thomas Aquinas shows an evolution of his thought which reached a culmination in the *Summa*. In this monumental work Aquinas follows Scripture: "Since in Scripture everywhere the reason for the incarnation is assigned to the sin of the first man, it can be said more fittingly that the work of the incarnation was ordered by God as a remedy for sins so that if sin had not existed, there would not have been an incarnation."[10]

Duns Scotus, on the other hand, argues that the Incarnation should be considered apart from the need for redemption. The Incarnation of the Word was, first and foremost, the greatest work of God and should be seen antecedently to and independently of the prevision of sin. Redemption was predestined so that Christ could be the adorer and glorifier of the Holy Trinity, the reason for all things, the final and exemplary cause of all in the natural and supernatural world order, and finally so that he might be the universal mediator and mystical head of angels and men.[11]

Both opinions relate the Incarnation to the Second Person of the Blessed Trinity. While it is true that Aquinas derives his opinion, in part at least, from Scripture, and sees a redemptive Incarnation in the New Testament, at a more fundamental level he situates the Incarnation in the Trinity of Persons in God. In the all-knowing awareness of everything, God had foreseen from all eternity the fall of humankind and then from eternity predicated the Incarnation as a remedy for the fall. The scenario would appear to be the Three Persons in God anticipating the fall and providing the Incarnation as the remedy.

For Duns Scotus, Christ was primarily destined to be the adorer and glorifier of the Trinity. The work *ad extra* was an expression of the work *ad intra*. Since the Word was the reason for all things, the final and exemplary cause of all in the natural and supernatural world order, it was a necessary fulfillment of a reality in God that was the essential motivation for the Incarnation, not the historical fact of the fall.

ADORATION DUE TO THE HUMANITY OF JESUS

THE QUESTION of worship involves the appropriate relationship between creator and creature. In the context of this chapter, theologians discussed whether the worship that is due to God should be afforded as well to the humanity of Jesus. The conclusion, of course, was affirmative, since Jesus was seen as one person who is the self of the Logos. Such is the foundation for the worship due to the humanity of Jesus.[12] A further conclusion is that "on account of the hypostatic union of Christ's humanity with the Logos, it [the humanity] is to be reverenced with *latria,* the adoration due to God, in Itself although not for its own sake."[13]

THE ETHICAL PERFECTION OF JESUS

THE ETHICAL perfection of Jesus implies freedom from sin and the fullness of God's life within him, which is love. Theologians discussed the possibility of sin in the life of Jesus and concluded that Jesus was free from all original sin, from all concupiscence and from all personal sin. The arguments often refer to Scripture, but at a more fundamental level it would be impossible for Jesus to have the inclinations to sin from within because of the unity of his human and divine natures. With regard to temptation from without, the same argument was used. Jesus possessed "an innate substantial purity illuminating the whole man."[14]

If someone objected that in the gospel of Mark Jesus says that God alone is good (Mark 10:18), and contended that this implies, since Jesus clearly refused to be called good, that he recognized inadequacies in his own being, the response would often avoid the heart of the question: "But in this case he surely had his eye not so much on himself as upon the infinite perfection of God. And precisely because he was closer to God than any other creature, he saw deeper than our human eye into the depths of divine holiness. His human feeling was overawed by the sight of this glory which stood like an overwhelming light before his soul. Jesus could see this light more clearly than any other man."[15]

If the theology of Jesus is taken from above, as it is in this example, then all questions of sin and temptation must be considered as the possibility of sin on the part of the Second Person of the Blessed Trinity and the possibility of tempting the Logos. All such considerations come immediately to naught. When we read in Scripture of the cleansing of the temple, the cursing of the fig tree, the harsh words to his mother, Jesus' anger with the scribes and Pharisees, his condescending attitude toward the Canaanite woman, all of these must be explained away, since any sign of weakness or even imperfect moral dispositions cannot be ascribed to the person of Jesus. The Second Person of the Blessed Trinity cannot do anything that could be construed as less than what might be expected in polite society.[16] The model of the particular Christology will set the framework

within which all explanations will be found. Jesus had
to have the fullness of virtue which was the positive
side of his sinlessness. Anything less would be beneath
the dignity of the Second Person of the Blessed Trinity.

THE ENTRANCE OF JESUS INTO HISTORY

THE ENTRANCE of Jesus into human history[17] raises
many questions regarding the virginal conception, the
relationship of Jesus to Joseph and of Joseph to Mary,
the role of the Holy Spirit and the Father. In the traditional understanding, Jesus enters into human history
through the full paternity of God the Father, without
any human paternity. Theologians talk about the *tran-
situs* of the Son of God from the divine sphere into the
human. In the divine sphere he remains the Logos and
Son, but by his entrance into our human dimension he
becomes man, assuming a historicity so that he is a
human being within human history. The activity was
seen as primarily that of God who is Father, but not
without the involvement of the other persons of the
Trinity. All that was created, and especially humankind,
was created through the Word in the Spirit, so that in
the Spirit all things participate in the Word, but the history of God's dealings with people is further evolved
into historical stages. In these steps the one that is the
most important is the entrance of the Son into history.

Humankind had experienced sin in spite of the plan
of God to destine all to happiness. With the advent of
sin God had to establish his plan anew through the
sending of his Word. Thus, the Father sent his Son as
the Word of God incarnate. While it is primarily the
work of the Father, it is also the *kenosis* (emptying)
of the Son. Jesus as the Word Incarnate entered sinful
flesh that he might bear the sins of the world and bring
forgiveness and salvation.

One result of this line of reflection is the belief that
Mary, the Mother of Jesus, was a virgin. That Jesus

could not have been God's Son if he had been conceived as any other human being is not immediately evident, but if you begin with the thought of the paternity of the Father in the Trinity as the source of the Son, then it is a natural conclusion that Jesus had to be born of a virgin. There is no need for further paternity, since it already exists in the relationship between Father and Son. The model of Jesus as the Second Person of the Blessed Trinity gives support to the doctrine of virginal conception just as the dogma of virginal conception supports the belief that Jesus was the Second Person of the Blessed Trinity.

Christian attitudes toward sexuality have not always been very positive. If in truth Jesus was the incarnation of the Word of God, the Son, then some believers wished to separate him from all taint of sexuality. The conclusion, at least on the levels of piety, was that Jesus was somehow more perfect in being if he was disassociated from human sexuality. Little thought was given to the implications of this line of reasoning for the true humanity of Jesus. The model of Jesus also affected the understanding of sexuality in Christian tradition. The entrance of the Logos into history was based solely upon his relationship to God, thus avoiding any human paternity; this view cast a shadow over the positive value of human generation. It also had implications for the doctrine of the perpetual virginity of Mary.

The doctrine of the virginal conception is very old in Christian tradition. Even before the year 200, the affirmation of belief in Christ Jesus was expanded in the old Roman Creed by a reference to his birth from the Virgin Mary in order to counteract a Docetism and Gnosticism that questioned the reality of the humanity of Jesus.[18] The Nicene Creed also affirmed a virginal conception. In all of these instances, however, we should recall that the whole question of the relationship of the humanity and divinity of Jesus was being hotly debated during this period. The Church tried to pre-

serve both the divinity and the humanity of Christ in
the face of heresies. In such a situation the symbol of
the Virgin Mary was ideal, since it allowed one to
emphasize "virgin" to preserve the divinity while stress-
ing that Mary was a woman to preserve the true humanity. In any case, the prime model was the Second
Person of the Blessed Trinity, who was the Logos that
had become man.

The gospels of Matthew and Luke also speak of a
virginal conception, even if these accounts need to be
nuanced.[19] There is no doubt that the writers of these
gospels presented a virginal conception even, if their
motivation owed more to a contemporary controversy
than to an effort to establish a dogmatic formulation.[20]
In this work I am more concerned with the use of a
model than the actual scriptural or theological foundations for the doctrine as expounded by the model. Using
a different model may still preserve the virginity of
Mary, but with a slightly different understanding of the
truth contained in the teaching.

THE ACTIVITIES AND WORKS OF JESUS

IN TRADITIONAL Christology, the activities and works
of Jesus involved those actions in his ministry that
might be considered *theandric* (coming from the divine person): miracles and prophecies. Many theologians would divide the activities of Jesus into those
which are truly *theandric* (miracles and prophecies)
and the daily activities of his life, which are called
theandric acts only in the widest use of that term.

The medieval theologians proposed the principle that
actions belong to the person (*actiones sunt supposi-
torum*) and derive from his essence (*actiones sequun-
tur esse*). As a result of these principles, all of the activities are predicated of the person of Jesus, which is the
divine person of the Word. The Word of God, the eternal Son, raised Lazarus from the tomb, and the Word

of God wept because Lazarus was dead; the Word of God prophesied that Peter would deny him three times, and the Word of God washed the feet of Peter.[21]

When we examine the activities of Jesus such as eating and drinking, sleeping and walking, these actions are truly human, but since Jesus the man is the divine person of the Word, these actions would also be called divine by reason of being acts of a divine person. When we use the model of the Second Person of the Blessed Trinity for our theology, we have to view all of the actions of Jesus as divine actions, since we are directed to the person of the Word which is the foundation for all actions.

Traditional apologetics developed further, to the point of asserting an obligation to believe in the divinity of Jesus. If Jesus performed miracles and uttered prophecies, then these actions manifested to all that we are face to face with more than just an ordinary human being. We are dealing with a divine person.[22] A theologian could read the gospels which speak of the amazement of the listeners: "Never did man speak as this man (Matt. 13:27)" and conclude that: "Expressions like these, of which there are many in the gospels, show that those who knew Christ beheld the deeds he performed in his human nature, realized that he was not just human. They realized that his human nature lay mysteriously but firmly rooted in a Person who was far above anything human as to be divine."[23] Once an individual realized the presence of such divine activities which were not opposed to human reason, there was an obligation to believe in Jesus as divine. All of this was rooted in the person of the Word, which formed the paradigm for any understanding of the activities of Jesus in his ministry.

This tendency to go to the root cause also affects the chief redemptive activity of the Lord: his cross and resurrection. Since this was the activity of the Word of God, it has an infinite value for redemption. We can say, "God died on the cross, but solely in so far as he was a man, and as only the Person of the Word became man, only the Person of the Word died on the Cross."[24]

Further speculation on the value of any activity of Jesus concluded that any act of Jesus would be sufficient to redeem humankind, because it was the activity of the Word. The shedding of blood at the circumcision was an activity which, since it was rooted in the person of the Word, could be sufficient for the redemption of all. To die a human death was a decision on the part of the Word of God, but this activity was in no way necessary for the salvific power of redemption.[25]

The apocryphal gospels demonstrate that he could work any miracles he wished at any period of his life. Theologians saw him as the Word of God walking around in the body of a child, living out a scenario that had been foreseen and preordained. If all is rooted in the Second Person of the Blessed Trinity, then there is no other way to understand the activities of Jesus other than that of a divine person who is expressing himself in human actions.

Traditional theology understood all of this through instrumental causality. Again it was Thomas Aquinas who gave the clearest philosophical foundation for these ideas.[26] An instrument which an artist uses produces an artistic result only if it is closely controlled and united to the artist. The control of the instrument by the artist does not deprive the instrument of its own specific activity nor of its contribution to the final effect produced. Rather, the effect comes simultaneously from the principal cause, the artist, and from the instrumental cause (secondary cause), the material used.

We can apply these notions to Jesus and see that the humanity is a conjoined instrument. It preserves its own proper power in its activities and has distinctive characteristics, but the principal cause is always the person of the Word. This explains the theological understanding

f all of the activities of Jesus, even the most ordinary,
s *theandric,* even if some of them are *theandric* only in
 wide sense, since all are referred to the principal
ause, the person of the Word.

THE KNOWLEDGE OF JESUS

HE QUESTION of the knowledge and consciousness of
esus figures more prominently than all of the other
actors that we have mentioned in any discussion of the
nfluence of a paradigm on Christology.[27] The Third
Council of Constantinople defined as a truth of faith
he existence of two activities in Jesus, divine and
uman. As a result, theologians—especially during the
Middle Ages—developed the theories of two kinds of
nowledge: human and divine. As God, Jesus possessed
he divine knowledge of God proper to each person of
he Blessed Trinity; as man, he also possessed human
nowledge and the human way of knowing common to
ll people. By his divine knowledge, Jesus knew God in
imself and all other things in God. This divine knowl-
dge was the uncreated knowledge of the Word, equal
o that of the Father and of the Holy Spirit.

The human knowledge of Jesus was essentially
ifferent from the divine knowledge and can be further
istinguished. Firstly, from the very moment of his con-
eption, Jesus' humanity enjoyed the beatific vision.
This knowledge belonged to his humanity by reason of
he hypostatic union. Thus, Jesus had a human knowl-
dge of his divine being and personality; he always had
his knowledge, which the saints enjoy in heaven, in the
ighest possible intensity. Secondly, Jesus' mind was
lso endowed with infused knowledge; he knew, as
reated spirits know, all that was equal to him and infe-
ior to him as human and he had, moreover, some
nowledge about God himself more perfect than any
vhich a person has by nature. Finally, as man, Jesus
ad ordinary acquired and empirical knowledge, which

he gained from his contact with others and his earthly experience.

Some might think so complex a set of distinctions would reflect a real division in Jesus himself, but provided we recall that one person is the source of these types of knowledge we should not be dismayed at such an analytical approach. As God Jesus knew all things and as man Jesus saw all things in God. As recently as 1947 Pope Pius XII wrote in *Mystici Corporis*, "He also enjoys the beatific vision in a degree, both as regards extent and clarity, surpassing that of the saints in heaven."[28] When some have objected that such a vision is incompatible with the suffering described in the gospels, theologians have often turned to a physical example to help to understand the combination of suffering and a beatifying vision: "A storm can lash the sides of a mountain and let loose on it rain and hail and lightning. But nothing disturbs the peace of the mountain heights."[29]

While the Church has never defined that Christ had infused knowledge, it is a conclusion that must follow from the model of Christology that sees Jesus as part of the Trinity. Jesus should have infused knowledge since he is the Second Person of the Blessed Trinity; he should also know more than any angel or any saint or any doctor of the Church. Such knowledge would be independent of any human experience. The only limitation placed upon this type of knowledge is the possibility of advertence: "His human mind did not always advert to all that it knew and at any one moment of his human life this knowledge must have been, as we say, latent within his mind and available to use when needed."[30]

Again, Thomas Aquinas took the lead in the discussion of acquired knowledge. He wanted to preserve the full humanity of Jesus and all of his natural activities, and thus Aquinas maintained a human acquired knowledge. He argued that the perfection of Christ's acquired knowledge had to befit his mission and no doubt our Lord himself set out to acquire such knowledge. The question of resolving this acquired knowledge with infused knowledge was never adequately answered. Aquinas referred to the difference between habit and action, which, in my opinion, no theologian has ever been able to explain.[31] We can conclude that many theologians contended that Jesus had an encyclopedic type of knowledge. He knew all things in God while he also had acquired knowledge. The infused knowledge was present when he needed it.

In the history of Christology since the Council of Chalcedon this model has had a significant effect on all of theology. If the foundation for the understanding of Jesus is the person of the Word, then the motive for the incarnation, the infirmities and weaknesses of Jesus' humanity, his entrance into history, his activities and works and, finally, his knowledge and consciousness, will all be understood only in relationship to the divinity of the person. More generally, the theological conclusions and pronouncements of the official Church have all been influenced by this overriding model.

The final aspect of Christology, which is also the culmination of Jesus' life, is his resurrection. Although this is the keystone of Christology,[32] the resurrection did not figure prominently in the Christology based on the model of the Second Person of the Blessed Trinity. If we have the person of the Word responsible for all of the activities of the earthly life of Jesus, then, as the Word of God, Jesus raised himself from the grave. This miracle was seen as the greatest of Jesus' miracles, proving to all who would listen that in truth Jesus was the divine Son of God. In the history of Christology this event in the life of Jesus was related to his other miracles and understood as merely the natural outcome of his divine nature. The eternal Word became man, was aware of his divinity even as he lived his human life, performed actions which belonged properly to the

Second Person of the Blessed Trinity, understood completely his mission and, finally, after he had finished his task on earth and had been crucified, rose from the dead to prove to all the truth of his mission and person. In this view Christology must always take as its starting point the existence of the Second Person of the Blessed Trinity. Only in this way can we understand the meaning of Jesus of Nazareth.

In later chapters of this book I shall deal similarly with the problems associated with the other models of Christology. I have begun with this model since, for most Christians, and Roman Catholics in particular, it has been the dominant model for several centuries and has influenced all of the catechisms down to the present time. Even developments since the Second Vatican Council have not completely altered this position.

For Protestant theologians this has not always been the case. The last hundred years have witnessed many models for Jesus, which have been explored in a plethora of books. Often enough it was up to the individual Protestant theologian to choose among the many approaches to Jesus that were presented in scholarly circles and develop a Christology accordingly. At the same time, it is evident from the writings on the subject that the earlier conciliar definitions had an important influence on the majority of Protestant theologians after the period of Liberal Protestantism in the nineteenth century.[33] Karl Barth, for example, in his *Church Dogmatics* relies heavily on conciliar Christology. Thus the model can be evaluated with implications for all of Christian theology.

No doubt, such an approach has clear and distinct advantages. The advantages can be summarized accordingly:

Firstly, for Roman Catholics, this has been the approach of the official Church, as can be witnessed in recent documents and traced back to the early councils. Since the Roman Church, unlike its Protestant counterparts, claims that its distinct teaching authority is founded on divine revelation, it is difficult for any member of that communion to maintain a different position from what official teaching affirms. The result is a clear Christology that can be easily presented in official documents with the firm support of centuries of tradition. In times of great social upheaval and of new developments in all aspects of life, the believer feels comfortable in subscribing to a clear Christology which has such a backing. Even if a Roman Catholic would like to take a new look at such a model, it could prove embarrassing to have to deal with unequivocal Church statements. This results in a uniformity in understanding the meaning of Jesus. Even in the study of Jesus in scholarly circles such a model imposes a sense of order, and sets the parameters within which the theologian may develop new ideas.

The second advantage is that this approach is clearly *theandric:* the model preserves the divinity of Jesus and protects it against any attempts to denigrate or discredit it. Over the course of centuries individuals have attempted to rethink the meaning of Jesus in ways that resulted in a loss or, at any rate, a lessening of any sense of the divine. The period of Liberal Protestantism in the late nineteenth century and the Modernist crises of the Roman Catholic tradition at the turn of this century both demonstrate how certain kinds of rethinking of Christology can lessen the sense of the divinity of Jesus. The more recent Death of God theology has led to similar results. If the model is the Second Person of the Trinity there is no possibility of the divinity of Jesus being lessened, forgotten or lost.

A third advantage is the theological elaboration that can be built upon this model. Everyone tends to seek unity in life and in thought. This is particularly true when we are trying to deal with a sense of mystery. Previously we noted that with Jesus we face inexhaustible intelligibility, but if we can find a cohesive model that will order this intelligibility, then we can be more secure in our theology. The model of the Second Person of the Blessed Trinity gives a cohesiveness and stability that clarifies the mission of Jesus, his miracles and prophecies, his knowledge and resurrection as well as his entrance into history. If all is rooted in the eternity of God then all of the minor aspects of the life of Jesus can be ordered according to one principle. This abstract Christology becomes the basis for the concrete Christology of the gospels and gives a theological principle that can be applied in every case. The model also affects other questions of theology—for example, those related to the institutional Church or to principles of morality. The model of the Second Person of the Trinity offers an omniscient God/man directing things to his purpose. An ecclesiology based on this model tends to share in this omniscience, giving clear, objective principles of moral conduct. Jesus spoke authoritatively to his Church for all times and circumstances since he spoke from the eternity of God. Jesus foresaw his Church with its sacramental system and positions of authority and affirmed the entire process based upon his decision and knowledge as the Second Person of the Trinity. The Church's theology followed suit.

Without discounting the advantages of such an approach to Jesus, it must be admitted that it also labors under several serious liabilities.

In the first place, in spite of efforts to prove the contrary, the model has only a meager basis in Scripture. Certainly the gospels present Jesus as the Son of God, but not as the all-knowing, beatified Christ of later theology. While the New Testament does speak of God as Father and Son and Spirit, it does not become philosophical in trying to distinguish persons and nature. The Jesus in the gospels appears more like a man of his own times and very unlike the Jesus of this model. The New Testament gives a foundation for the approach in its teaching on the special relationship to God as Father that Jesus experienced, but the differences in the various New Testament Christologies are often lost in the effort to spin out the theories of the relationship between humanity and divinity.

Secondly, the model tends to eclipse the meaning of the humanity of Jesus. No longer do we have an individual with human feelings, with hopes, expectations and needs, but the embodiment of the eternal Word. What is important is the "person" who is acting, the Second Person of God, rather than what is said or done. The notion of instrument can create the illusion that the Logos used the humanity of Jesus much as an artist would use a paintbrush or a piano to create a picture or music. With the tendency always to go to the divine source of all in Jesus, the reality of the human life of Jesus falls into shadows.

Thirdly, such an approach often stifles theology. For some, theology becomes an effort to give support to the statements of the official Church rather than an attempt to explore new avenues. A heavily metaphysical construct in Christology tends to impose its conclusions on other areas of theology as well. If we already know the answers in Christology, and these conclusions control other areas of theology, how can a theologian possibly break new ground? This Christology gives a foundation for attitudes within the Church which are not in keeping with the entire biblical tradition nor with the understandings that have developed since the Second Vatican Council. Theologians must be free to think. This model also limits the development of theology, since it presupposes that Jesus has already revealed all that is in any way necessary for the Church and the individual believer. It does not take into account the development of the behavioral sciences and their effects on theology. Rather it tends to close doors on areas of discussion instead of facilitating the efforts of theologians to grow in the understanding of faith and thus fulfill their responsibility in the Church.

Fourthly, this model is detrimental to Christian piety, since it can easily create a situation in which the ordinary believer cannot identify with Jesus, when always faced with the immediate claim that he functioned as the Second Person of the Blessed Trinity. If Jesus is the model for other fallible human beings to emulate, the model cannot be so separated from ordinary human experience that there is no hope for imitation. Jesus, even as a man, is elevated into the realm of the transcendent God, with little or no effect on the lives of believers other than to make them conscious of their sins.

Finally, this approach is not in tune with the developments in theology and in the Church in recent times. In an age of dialogue not only with Christian traditions but also with other religions, at a time when we are in need of a savior who can be part of the human experience and who presented himself as the humble carpenter of Nazareth, who came not to be served but to serve, who offered a sense of personal worth in his dealings with people, the emphasis on the Second Person of the Blessed Trinity as the paradigm for all Christology is unacceptable. When people are concerned principally not with the God question but with the question of the meaning of human life, at a time when this life is more precarious, it does little good to speak of an eternal "Logos" descending and living an unreal life, and hope at the same time to attract ordinary people to see their value in the light of this man's life. The Second Person of the Blessed Trinity may prove interesting to scholars in the history of Christianity, but offers little reason for enthusiasm to the person who lives in the throes of anxiety, searching to eke out some personal worth and meaning in a world gone mad with power.

In every age the Church maintains its tradition and still strikes out into new areas. It should not shrink from a task that calls out for new approaches and models. This does not mean that we have to throw out the advantages of this model for Jesus. If we keep in mind the sense of mystery that is expressed in Chapter 1 of this book, then we can keep the notion of Jesus as the preexistent Second Person of the Blessed Trinity within its proper bounds and can see to it that other models are not lost. In this way we will be able to realize that the many approaches to Jesus can enrich the Christian tradition, while taking only one approach impoverishes our understanding.

In spite of the strong emphasis on this model in the official teaching of the Church, other approaches were never completely forgotten. Even now the Church finds itself challenged to respond to the new models that are being offered by various theologians, which have grown out of their particular life experiences. These approaches affect the meaning of Jesus as the Second Person of the Blessed Trinity so that it is now difficult to see this model as a paradigm for Christology. One possible exception to this movement would be a strong reaction by conservatives to the humanizing of Jesus and thus a swing back to the more numinous, attempting to make this model, once again, the paradigm. For the present, however, other models have entered the scene with a vigor that cannot be gainsaid. It is to these models that we must turn if we are to appreciate more of the inexhaustible mystery that is Jesus of Nazareth.

NOTES

1. *The Pope Speaks,* vol. 17 (1972–73), 64–68.

2. See K. Rahner, *"Chalkedon . . ."*

3. For a general overview of this Council, any standard encyclopedia of theology is helpful. See *Sacramentum Mundi,* vol. 3 (New York: Herder and Herder, 1969), pp. 201–3; also, A. Greilmeier, *Christ in Christian Tradition* (London: Mowbray, 1965).

4. See *Teachings of the Catholic Church,* pp. 151–53.

5. *Ibid.* This formulation by Leo became the foundation for the debate during the Council of Chalcedon, as well as for the Council of Ephesus, which ended in disarray.

6. *Ibid.*, pp. 153–54. As a result of this formulation, most Christians are aware of the statement regarding two natures in one person, but are not aware of the controversy surrounding the formulation.

7. *Ibid.*, pp. 169–70. The debate at the Third Council of Constantinople preserved the human will of Jesus and human operations. If this had not been formulated, the humanity could easily have been absorbed in the divinity.

8. Greilmeier, p. 492. This authoritative study on the history of Christological controversy is invaluable, even though I cannot agree that the Jesus of the New Testament can be heard with undiminished strength in the philosophical discussions.

9. See *Dictionnaire de théologie catholique*, VII, 1466–1511. Also see K. Rahner, *Foundations of Christian Faith*, pp. 214 ff. Since the main concern was the theology of the Trinity and the Three Persons were seen as equal in all things, it would be a logical conclusion that, although any of the Three Persons could have become incarnate, it was fitting that it was the Word, since the Word proceeded directly from the Father.

10. *Summa Theologica*, III, q. 1, a. 3.

11. *Reportata Parisiensia*, 3, dist. 7, 1, 3 and 4.

12. K. Adams, *The Christ of Faith* (New York: Pantheon, 1957), p. 24. See also M. Scheeben, *The Mysteries of Christianity* (St. Louis: Herder, 1946), p. 331. "It [the humanity] participates in the nature of the divinity." Accordingly, then, the humanity will receive the adoration due to the divinity.

13. *Ibid.*, p. 240. Also Scheeben, pp. 329–30, 332. "For the anointing of Christ is nothing less than the fullness of the divinity of the Logos, which is substantially joined to the humanity and dwells in it incarnate."

14. *Ibid.*, p. 246.

15. *Ibid.*, p. 247.

16. *Ibid.*, pp. 247–54. The efforts to reinterpret the gospels to avoid any act by Jesus that would be considered less than perfect has a long tradition. The early Fathers of the Church were also quick to offer explanations for his cursing the fig tree, the harsh words to the Canaanite woman, etc.

17. See R. Brown, *The Virginal Conception and the Bodily Resurrection of Christ* (New York: Paulist, 1973).

. See: J.N.D. Kelly, *Early Christian Creeds* (London: ngman, 1960), pp. 144–45.

. Brown, *The Virginal Conception . . .* , pp. 52–68.

. Brown has argued convincingly that the origin of this dition comes from the accusation by Jews that Jesus was egitimate. See *The Birth of the Messiah* (New York: oubleday, 1977), 28–29, 142–43, 150, 534–42.

. F. Ferrier, *What is the Incarnation?* (New York: awthorne, 1962), p. 158. This is a popularization of the incipal theological positions held by most Christologists up til the very recent past. See M. Scheeben, p. 330: "In its vn actions the humanity becomes the *instrumentum con-*nction of this divine person and these actions themselves ereby receive an infinite dignity and efficacy—in a word, an finite value." See also E. Mersch, *The Theology of the ystical Body* (St. Louis: Herder, 1951), pp. 229 ff.

.. Ferrier, p. 159. See also Mersch, p. 228: "The incarna-on established a new human species, or rather effected a newal of the species: Divinized humanity."

. Ferrier, p. 159.

-. Ferrier, p. 160. The traditional understanding of the ommunication of idioms" allows us to say that God died the cross but not that divinity died on the cross.

. Rahner would disagree with this opinion. For him, Jesus d to die to achieve redemption. See *Theology of Death* New York: Herder and Herder, 1961). Mersch would aintain a similar position for different reasons. See *The heology of the Mystical Body*, p. 285: "The God-man by ing the God-man in the sinful humanity is intrinsically the deemer consecrated to death; conversely by being the deemer who died on the cross, He emerges most clearly as e God-man in sinful humanity."

. *Summa Theologica*, III, q. 19, a. 1.

'. For a general summary of the question with appropriate bliography, see my *Jesus, Lord and Christ,* Chapter 4.

. Pope Pius XII, *Mystici Corporis,* paragraph 48.

. M. Vigue, *Le Christ* (Paris, 1947), p. 571.

. Ferrier, p. 169. The popularization of these theories en-uraged Christians to believe that Jesus knew everything at would happen to him as well as to everyone else. Even there could be limitations on infused knowledge (most of e time there were not), Jesus, as the divine person, always d divine knowledge.

31. *Summa Theologica*, III, q. 12, a. 2.

32. Again, a general summary on contemporary resurrectic
theology can be found in my *Jesus, Lord and Christ*.

33. For a good summary of the weaknesses of Liberal Pro
estantism of the nineteenth century, see Barth, *The Huma
ity of God*, pp. 11–33. The author reacted strongly agair
this tendency; from this reaction came the rebirth of a tra
scendent theology in Protestantism.

3

THE MYTHOLOGICAL CHRIST

ᴛᴏ ᴄʜᴏᴏꜱᴇ ᴛᴏ make the second chapter of this work an analysis of the various attempts to demythologize Jesus may seem strange, but the contrast with the preceding chapter is so striking as to make it an important stage in the development of a theory of models.

Since the publication of J.A.T. Robinson's book *Honest to God*[1] in 1963, many Scripture scholars and some theologians have readily accepted the mythological character of some aspects of traditional Christianity and Christology. They do not reject the historical Jesus, but they have reexamined some of the tenets of traditional Christology. Our portrait of the historical Jesus has been colored by the faith experience of the early followers, and thus we should not be alarmed if some aspects of this historical Jesus have been lost in the Christ of faith. The study of the mythological Christ is an effort to ask the real Jesus of Nazareth to stand forth. In the history of studies of this question, startling conclusions abound.

Over the two thousand years of Christianity there have always been skeptics who have claimed that the Christian religion is more the result of human ingenuity and imagination than of any divinely inspired founder. Often the skeptics reject Jesus as a historical figure; at the most, they consider him as a real person who suffered from illusions. For others, his historicity is not as important as his meaning. In the opinion of these people, Jesus, like the Greek gods of old, performed function as a representative person, which is more important than the question of his historical reality.

Recently a group of Anglican theologians published collection of essays examining traditional Christology. They presuppose that by now Christians have overcome the outdated notion that Jesus was in truth the Incarnation of the Son of God and they try to discover the reason that gave birth to such an idea. The book, *The Myth of God Incarnate*[2] uses the word myth in the sense of something that is not true, and thus they try to get to the real meaning of Jesus, discarding the accretions that have overlaid the historical Jesus.

In the course of centuries, the word "myth" has developed both positive and negative meanings for different thinkers. In this chapter we shall combine many different approaches to Jesus under the rubric "the Mythological Christ." In some instances, as shall be clear, myth is something positive and truthful; in other instances myth implies just the opposite. The common element that binds these various theologies together is the conviction that the Jesus presented in traditional Christology is not the real Jesus of Nazareth. To understand the various positions presented today, we need a sketch of biblical criticism over the past two hundred years.

Until the end of the eighteenth century the gospels were accepted at their face value as a description, written by eyewitnesses or their associates, of the person, life and teachings of Jesus of Nazareth. The gospels were historically accurate and could be accepted as authentic and truthful. In 1774, however, G. E. Lessing published posthumous selections from the manuscript of a colossal work by H. S. Reimarus, who had died a few years previously. This began the controversy which has yet to lose any of its force.[3]

Reimarus believed that Christianity rests upon

...d. According to his theory, Jesus was a Jew, steeped ...Jewish tradition and thus anti-Gentile, who did not ...h to found a new religion but to deepen the old one. ...may have healed some people, but he never per-...med any prodigious miracles. He was a messiah who ...ected a popular uprising that would allow him to ...d the revolt against the pro-Roman Pharisees and ...hedrin. Unfortunately for Jesus, this uprising never ...terialized and he was condemned to death. Then ...ne Christianity.

...he disciples of Jesus, according to Reimarus, ...ated Christianity out of their sense of disap-...ntment. Jesus himself had expected the kingdom of ...d to come in his lifetime and never said anything ...ut dying and rising. As a result of his death, the dis-...les fell back on the secondary aspect of Jewish apoc-...ptic hopes and transferred the kingdom to a super-...ural sphere as found, for example, in chapters 7 and ...f Daniel. They gathered followers who believed that ...us was the Davidic messiah and invented the resur-...tion. To give substance to their claims they stole the ...ly of Jesus, waited fifty days for it to decompose and ...n declared him to be the awaited messiah. Chris-...ity rests upon a fraud. Jesus Christ is mythological ...a negative sense, since he never existed as presented ...the gospels. He did not preach the good news as ...orded by the evangelists; he did not rise from the ...d and is surely not the Son of God.

...he interest in rationalism in the nineteenth century ...o contributed to a skeptical attitude toward Jesus and ...ristianity. Many Christian thinkers, influenced by ra-...nalism but eager to maintain the value in Chris-...nity, reexamined the gospels as well as the history of ...ristianity and tried to preserve what was most essen-...l to Christian faith. Once again, it was the Christol-...y that was most greatly modified.

...D. F. Strauss was the first to deal specifically with the ...estion of myth, and gave his own definition.[4] For

Strauss, myth was the clothing in historical form
religious ideas, shaped by the unconsciously inventi
power of legend and embodied in a historical perso
Before Strauss, certain rationalists had labeled the bir
and resurrection of Jesus as legend and myth, but wi
Strauss we get a consistent theory. He suggested th
miracles also derive from legend: the stories of t
transfiguration and resurrection, as well as the bir
narratives and much of what is extraordinary in t
gospels can be attributed to this human tendency
glorify a man after death. Theologians must study Jes
to remove the mythological elements and then discov
the true Jesus. Myth is negative, a hindrance to tr
faith that should be examined and discarded.

A third individual of the same period who drew ce
tain of the premises of his predecessors to their logic
conclusions was Bruno Bauer.[5] His ideas developed
three stages: first an ultra-Strauss period in which
deals with the concept of myth but replaces the ter
with "reflection"; a second period characterized by
questioning of the historical Jesus with the convictio
that it is the thought of Jesus that is important, and n
the man; finally, an outright denial of the historical pe
son of Jesus. Bauer concluded that Christianity is
compromise arising from the interchange between Jev
ish and Roman culture.

In the first period he studied the gospels beginnir
with John, working his way back to Mark and the hi
torical Jesus. For Bauer the gospel of John was a wor
of art, not a historical document, and was thorough
dominated by the creative reflection. Even Mark, tr
first gospel, could be considered a literary rather than
historical work. Thus we have the possibility that or
man invented the entire system of teachings, sinc
Matthew and Luke are expansions of Mark, and John
the result of the influence of Philo on the same bas
tradition.

In the second period of his theory's developmen

Bauer realized that it was necessary to free the theology of Jesus the messiah from the Judeo-Roman idol created by his followers. Whether Jesus existed or not is of no consequence, Bauer suggested: the higher religion associated with him is of value in itself. Christianity has merit because it encourages the overcoming of nature, not by self-alienation, but by penetrating and ennobling human life through a living out of the teachings of Christianity. There is myth involved in the gospels and in the portrait of Jesus, but this should not denigrate the importance that Christian values offer to life. Whether Jesus lived or not is of little consequence; what is important is the effect that Christianity can have on a person's life. Bauer came to believe that Jesus never did exist. He postulated the idea that some first-century A.D. thinkers cleverly created the Christian faith as a response to human need.

Today when people who are marginally acquainted with contemporary theology and scriptural studies hear of the word "myth," the name of Rudolf Bultmann immediately comes to mind.[6] This German hermeneute stamped twentieth-century biblical criticism with his own clear mark, and his thought will continue to influence developments for the next hundred years. Before Bultmann arrived on the scene (he was a prolific writer from 1920 to 1976) the stage had been set for his theories. He presented a new approach to the study of the New Testament by seeing "myth" not as something negative, but as something positive. Many people recognized the mythological elements in the gospels, but for now, for the first time, an interpreter of the New Testament saw a value in the myth as expressing a truth. Bultmann recognized the creative power of the early community; he questioned, on philosophical grounds, some of the supernatural elements of the New Testament; and finally, he had become disturbed by the inability of Christianity actually to minister to his contemporaries, especially during the First World War.

These influences formed the background for his lifelong study.

Bultmann studied the influence of Hellenism on the formation of the early preaching of Jesus and was eager to use some of the findings of contemporary philosophy, namely the existential approach of Martin Heidegger, in his study of the New Testament. All of these influences, as well as the development of the use of form criticism in the New Testament, laid the foundation for Bultmann's theology.

Immediately after the First World War, K. L. Schmidt, M. Dibelius and R. Bultmann applied a new method to the study of the Synoptics.[7] They were impressed by the efforts of H. Gunkel, who had examined the Old Testament to discover the various literary forms contained therein, and they sought to offer a similar study of the New Testament. Their theory postulates a period of oral transmission of the material contained in the synoptic gospels before it reached a written stage in Mark and in "Q" (the postulated written source used by Matthew and Luke in their composition). The oral tradition connected with Jesus assumed various literary genres or forms, each of which had its own history and its own life situation (*Sitz em Leben*) in the early Church, whether in Palestine or in the diaspora. The primitive community did not merely transmit the sayings of Jesus and his deeds; it adapted them to its own historical situation, created new ones and expressed them in particular literary forms. Hence the gospels are not accounts of what happened, but *kerygmatic* documents projected back into the life of Jesus. They tell us little, if anything, about the biography and personality of the historical Jesus.

Bultmann's theology is complicated and deals with many questions involving the use of philosophical principles of interpretation, the meaning of the Christian life, sin, faith, etc. For our purposes, we are concerned with two distinctive features of his thought: his concept of demythologizing and his understanding of Christology. Many people have their own peculiar understanding of myth, as we have already seen. The same is true for Bultmann. For him, meaning was more important than scientific understanding. Bultmann claimed to use myth in the historical and religious sense of the word, but with his own nuance.[8] Myth is the way of presenting things so that the otherworldly becomes worldly, the divine is seen in the human. Its meaning is positive and implies a direct activity of the divine, supernatural, superhuman, within the historical order. Divine or otherworldly activity is presented in analogy with human earthly activity.

An example of this application can be seen in his interpretation of miracles. According to Bultmann, a miracle is a happening among other happenings, and can be understood as the presence of the divine in human history only through the eyes of faith. When one believes, he or she can see the event as myth and recognize it as an act of God in human form. There may be a natural cause, but the event itself is interpreted from a theological perspective precisely because it is mythological.

Myth, as understood by Bultmann, will speak of God in human terms, especially when it depicts the use of power. In first-century culture there were clearly mythic elements that would have influenced Christianity. People viewed the universe as an edifice having three stories, with God in the heavens, people on earth and demons under the earth. This provided a basis for movement back and forth from earth to heaven, and from heaven to earth as well as for the entrance of demons into history, the exorcisms of Jesus, the atonement for sins which pleases a heavenly God, the Spirit of God coming from heaven to earth, the birth and resurrection of Christ, and so on.

Bultmann recognized the mythological elements that were prevalent in the first century and which colored the New Testament writings. He saw that in order to recognize the truth that was present in the myth, one had to get beyond the mythical reality to discover its meaning. He called this process "demythologizing." Such a process is not the denial of the truth or the value of the myth, nor is it a quantitative reduction of mythical representations; rather, it is a qualitative reinterpretation. Bultmann disagreed with Strauss, who had thought of myth as an allegory and differentiated the shell from the kernel, the latter being the great moral values that are contained in the myth. According to Bultmann, when Strauss and others applied this concept of myth to the New Testament, they actually destroyed the *kerygma,* since the preaching of Jesus is not found beside the myth but in the myth.

The *kerygma* is the saving act of God in Christ, which is expressed in the myths of the New Testament, such as miracles and resurrection. Demythologizing, then, is interpretation with no attempt on the part of the interpreter to eliminate the myth, but with an attempt to give an existential meaning to it. The true value of myth consists in the recognition that this world which lies before us is not its own ground and end. We are involved with powers, forces and values that cannot be communicated in any other way than in mythical language. What is significant is how individuals respond to the meaning that is expressed in the myth: how a person believes in Jesus and finds personal value in a commitment to him. What is communicated in myth is often much more than what can be communicated in strictly scientific language. That is the distinctive advantage of the mythological Christ.

CHRISTOLOGY

IN THE THOUGHT of Bultmann, Christ is the event of salvation, but this does not necessarily include the historical Jesus. Jesus proclaimed the kingdom of God, but in actuality the proclaimer became the proclaimed.[9] What is important in Christianity is not the how or the what of Jesus, but that Jesus was. Jesus himself has been mythologized into the Christ of faith. There was no point, for Bultmann, in trying to create a life of Jesus, since this has no relevance to the *kerygma*. He did not deny the historical Jesus, as other authors did, but it was clear that, in his thinking, the historical Jesus was not as important as the Christ of faith, the mythological Christ. We are dealing with an otherworldly reality that is being expressed in this-worldly terms, in a poetic and creative fashion.

This mythologizing embraced both Hellenistic as well as Jewish thought patterns, and so when we read the sayings of Jesus in the gospels we must distinguish three strata: the latest, which is Hellenistic; the Aramaic stratum, which is part of the experience of the earliest followers in an oral tradition; and the oldest, the pre-Aramaic stratum, from which most of the authentic sayings of Jesus arise.

Jesus of Nazareth, according to Bultmann, was an ordinary man—a Jew, not a Christian. What he preached was not identical with the earliest *kerygma* of Christianity. This primitive preaching was about Jesus as the Christ and depended on the experience of the Resurrection. This does not mean, however, that there is no continuity between the historical Jesus and the *kerygma*. Paul did not make up Christianity, as some have claimed, nor did anyone else. Jesus and Paul and other early Christian writers and preachers had the same basic teaching. Both Jesus and Paul appealed to people as sinners, asking for a decision about their personal existence. Bultmann proposed that we must do away with all messianic titles in the ministry of Jesus, since these are the creation of the early Church. There remains, however, an implicit Christology in the teaching of Jesus, even if it is not the *kerygma*. For Bultmann, this approach was actually legitimized in the

New Testament. Paul and John, for example, are no
interested in the historical Jesus, because they them
selves are concerned with the *kerygma*. The same ca
be said for the Synoptics.

If one were to have asked what is the difference be
tween the teaching of Jesus and the *kerygma*, Bultman
would have replied that the *kerygma* changes the one
time event of the historical Jesus into the once-for-al
Christ event—that is, the story of Jesus is considere
globally as the definitive eschatological event. Jesu
preached the coming of salvation and the *kerygm*
preached the salvation of God as already come in Jesu
the Christ.

To return to the meaning of demythologizing: the
meaning of Jesus as the Christ is translated into mytho
logical events and narratives which are meant to brin
people to a personal decision. The believer must mov
beyond the myth in order to appreciate the persona
presence of the saving God in his or her belief.

In this perspective, the Resurrection is the princi
pal myth. It has no historical value and it is not histori
cally verifiable, nor should anyone wish to verify it
What is important is the meaning that the Resurrectio
myth implies: God has given life to Jesus and made hin
his Christ; God will give life to anyone who responds ir
faith to the saving presence of God in history. The ob
jective event in faith is the Christ-event, in which indi
viduals come to understand that when they are weak
then God will act for them as he did for his Christ. Ir
the cross we see God's love and grace not as an emotior
(since we already know that God loves us) but as ar
act of grace from the almighty judge, for the sake o
the individual. The essence of the saving act is the grace
of God, which makes us surrender our attempts to real
ize ourselves on our own. This surrender is symbolized
by Jesus' death on the cross and permits a new exis
tence (resurrection). The Resurrection then becomes
fact—not in the historical sense, but only insofar as the

dividual person is changed by it existentially. The
resurrection does not mean the return to life of a dead
person, a resuscitated corpse, but involves faith. I accept the Resurrection as a sign of God's concern for
me. We can conclude that for Bultmann the individual's
self-understanding and the recognition that Jesus is the
Son of God were one and the same thing.[10]

Throughout this chapter we have examined the
model that presents Christ as mythological. We have already noted that there are several positions, from the
acceptance of Jesus as a historical figure, though mythologized into the Christ of Faith, to the denial of Jesus
as historical. Those who take the latter position define
the myth as a complete fabrication. Bultmann remained
somewhat suspended in his judgment here, maintaining
the historical reality of Jesus but emphasizing how little
import this has to faith. In Bultmann's opinion, the
early writers of the New Testament and the preachers
of the *kerygma* actually used another model: the gnostic redeemer myth. Bultmann's theology presupposes
knowing something about this gnostic myth. The gnostic redeemer myth cannot be explained succinctly because of the various expressions of Gnosticism that
were prevalent in the early centuries of Christianity.[11]
A summary of the myth as constructed by Bultmann includes the following: the primordial light had been
dispersed among human beings and the only way these
particles of light could be reunited was through the revelation of the truth, the *gnosis*, which was accomplished
by a particular individual who knew the truth and intro-
duced the initiates into it. With this as a background,
Bultmann believed, the early Christians adapted this
myth to fit the historical Jesus and thus the proclaimer
of the kingdom of God actually became the proclaimed.
The only fly in the anointment is our inability to discover such a myth prior to Christianity.

As should be evident, Bultmann used myth in a
specific way that differs from the popular understanding

of myth, which seems to equate it with what is fal
Bultmann recognized the mythological dress of
kerygma and sought to recover the preaching of Je
for twentieth-century believers. He turned to exist
tialism for the appropriate epistemological and pheno
enological categories to interpret the *kerygma* a
placed his emphasis on the Christ of Faith because
Jesus of history has been so overladen with mytholo
cal interpretation that it is difficult to recover any ac
rate information about the history of Jesus. Bultma
disavowed, then, any desire to recover the Jesus of I
tory. To do so, he believed, would reduce faith to
pendence on some kind of viable objective eviden
and this in turn would destroy the very meaning
faith. Christ is mythological for good reason.

At the outset of this chapter reference was made
the recent work of Anglican theologians, *The Myth*
God Incarnate. They also speak of myth, but in
different sense from Bultmann. In considering th
writings, we return to a negative understanding
myth, which calls into question the central affirmat
of Christology: Was Jesus in truth the incarnation
the Son of God? The reason for such a question g
back to the concerns of the nineteenth-century
tionalists, who concluded that no serious thinker co
assume that what our ancestors believed was in fac
truth that could hold its ground in the face of phi
sophical and scientific progress.

Michael Goulder begins his essay in this collect
with an anecdote which deserves a chuckle from ev
the most traditional of Christologists:

A few years ago the philosopher in my departme
who delights to pull the theologian's leg, asked me
I had heard the one about the Pope being told by
cardinals that the remains of Jesus had been dug
in Palestine. There was no doubt that it was Jesu
all the Catholic archeologists were agreed. "Oh," s
the Pope. "What do we do now?" "Well," said

cardinals, "there is only one hope left; there is a
Protestant in America called Tillich; perhaps you
could get him on the phone?" So Tillich was tele-
phoned and the position was explained to him. There
was a long pause, after which the voice said, "You
mean to say he really existed?"[12]

Similar anecdotes have been heard even in the clois-
ed halls of Roman Catholic as well as Protestant
minaries. It is not that people who had believed no
nger believe, but rather that their belief is in need of
thinking. After the years of questioning, every serious
nker has to deal with the problem of the mythologi-
. origins of Jesus, and in The Myth of God Incarnate
rious theories are proffered to explain the origin of
e doctrine of the incarnation. We have moved beyond
e question of the mythological Jesus to seek the expla-
tion for the development of the myth.

The Myth of God Incarnate concludes that there is
one explanation for the development of the myth of
e incarnation. The authors believe that the particular
igious, cultural and philosophical atmosphere of soci-
, both Jewish and Hellenistic, was conducive to the
velopment of such an idea, and they suggest that we
ll find the explanation of the doctrine in the general
nchretistic state of religion in the period. The authors
ached this conclusion because no one has found a sin-
e exact analogy to the total Christian claim about
sus in material that is definitely pre-Christian. We can
scover full-scale redeemer myths after Jesus, but not
fore. The figure of Jesus was the means of crystal-
ing elements which already existed in the religious
d intellectual milieu. According to F. Young, a con-
butor to The Myth of God Incarnate, there seem to
ve been four basic elements:

The use of phrases like "Son of God," with a wide
nge of implications, was current; these were applied
both human and superhuman beings.

2. The apotheosis or ascent of an exceptional man
the heavenly realm was found in both Jewish a
Greek traditions.

3. Belief in heavenly beings or intermediaries, some
whom could descend to help humankind and others
whom could act in judgment or in creation, was wi
spread.

4. A manifestation of the chief of these heavenly bei
in an incarnation is found in Hellenism as well as
Jewish theological speculation.[13]

If one studies these elements already found in Jew
and Greek thought, the similarity to the develop
Christian teaching on Jesus becomes apparent. There
however, one element of caution. What is also part
the Christian belief is its staunch adherence to the m
who was crucified under Pontius Pilate. The orthod
understanding of incarnation has always been firn
anchored in history, despite the objections of many h
torical skeptics. No wonder early Christianity had
struggle against Docetism and Gnosticism and the va
ous heresies that have plagued two thousand years
tradition. As long as the mythological was part of t
preaching, it would be difficult to prevent the devel
ment of unorthodox Christologies. As long as the ent
belief was rooted in history, the mythological eleme
could never claim complete ascendency.

For many people who believe in Jesus and in Ch
tianity, the mythological, in any sense, is completely u
acceptable. The authors who contributed to *The My
of God Incarnate* claim to be still Christian,[14] as o
Bultmann. To accept the mythical element in Christ
ogy does not imply a total rejection of faith. In fa
there are many advantages to using the mythologi
model for a personal Christology.

Firstly, the mythological model affirms the close re
tionship between Christianity and the environment o

which it arose. We cannot understand the writings of New Testament unless we understand the writings 1 the implicit expectations of the Old Testament and ecially the speculation on Jewish Wisdom. The same rue for Hellenism. There existed a developing matrix the ancient Near East comprised of a mixture of phi- ophy, religion and cultural elements that interacted 1 modified each other over a period of several hun- :d years. These concurrent influences did not develop a vacuum, but were the result of the contact of the man spirit with various human cultures. The hopes 1 aspirations expressed in the Greek myths were not lated from the human needs of the times, nor did the rs and anxieties expressed in the same myths spring t of a set of theories. When Christianity arose, it nd some basis in the expressed hopes and expecta- ns of the mass culture and thus it accepted some of t culture's mythical elements.

Secondly, the acceptance of this model of Jesus as a ythical" figure reminds Christians that there are ne elements in Christology that cannot and should t be taken as absolutes. The Christians of every age ve to deal with the meaning of Jesus, and they use terminology and the experience of the times to ex- ss their understanding of the Lord. To recall that re is such a thing as a mythological model of Jesus ninds theologians as well as believers that some as- cts of Christology are time-conditioned.

Thirdly, the value of Bultmann's as well as other ologians' approach is that it moves from a theoretical derstanding of Jesus to an existential one. Bultmann pastor tried to adapt Christianity to the needs of his low believers at a time when religion was considered elevant. He wanted to care for the needs of believers d thus his method of demythologizing was not meant downgrade Christian faith but to seek new expres- ns and possibilities for the contemporary mind.[15] The

mythological model gives a fluidity of approach to Jes
that can accommodate various levels of personal p
ception of the value of Christianity. The scientific mi
as well as the philosophical spirit can find comfort in

Fourthly, the mythological model releases dog
from the rigidity that has often characterized faith f
mulations. *The Myth of God Incarnate* is direct e
dence of the freedom that is afforded theologians if th
accept the mythological model, even if, in the pres
case, this freedom has gone too far in discarding
Christian doctrine of the incarnation altogether.

The drawbacks of such a model, however,
equally evident. The most serious concern is the co
plete divorcing of the historical Jesus from the Christ
Faith. After more than a hundred years of research
the question,[16] we have finally come to the point whe
the majority of scholars carefully point out the cl
relationship between the two, in spite of all of the
velopments that took place in the early Church's proc
mation of Jesus. The mythological model disregards t
relationship that must exist between the Jesus of histo
and the Christ of Faith.

Secondly, the mythological element relativizes Chr
tianity to an extreme degree. If we have Christian
based upon a mythical Christ of Faith, then there
no particular boundaries that can be ascribed to Chr
tianity. Without a foundation, Christianity not only c
develop in several directions, but will itself beco
shaky. We have already experienced the fragmenti
of Christianity. Such a model would only encoura
greater fragmentation, which would inevitably contr
ute to a process of internal disintegration.

Thirdly, the mythological model could cause serio
problems for the theological enterprise. Theology is t
human effort to understand faith and will survive as
contribution to faith only if it takes into considerati
the need of the human spirit to seek not only guidan

ut some element of stability. To rely solely upon a mythological model removes any sense of stability.

Finally, the model of Jesus as mythological figure calls into question the very truth of Christianity. Such a model has actually led to the denial of the historical Jesus and the assertion that Christian faith is founded on a fraud. Certainly this need not be the case, however, since we have examples of believers who accept the mythical elements and still maintain their Christian beliefs and values. The model, while it answers many of the contemporary questions, does not answer all of them.

Many valuable insights have accrued to the study of the New Testament as well as Christology when the mythological elements are accepted. No serious thinker can reject or consider unimportant the work of the critical scholars of the past century, and in particular the work of Rudolf Bultmann in the twentieth century. We have learned much from the efforts of these scholars. At the very least, they have made more traditional Christologists aware of the relativity that has always existed in our theological tradition. Roman Catholic theologians, who in the past were often too influenced by official pronouncements and traditional approaches, should find the mythological model of particular value. Roman Catholic theology has nothing to fear from the studies of Reimarus, Bauer, Strauss, Bultmann and others. True scholarship has always included in its purview insights that are considered valuable to the development of theology. Where would we be in our study of the Bible without the findings of archaeology, the historical-critical approach of the nineteenth century, and the development of biology, anthropology and psychology? All of these initially caused concern for traditional Christians but eventually benefited theology. For this reason there can never be a complete dismissal of the mythological school. Its truth can be of great assistance

to the traditional school, just as the reflective tradition
theologian can be of assistance to the more mytholog
cal-minded.

NOTES

1. J.A.T. Robinson, *Honest to God* (Philadelphia: Wes
minster, 1963), pp. 24–48.

2. John Hick, ed., *The Myth of God Incarnate* (Phila
delphia: Westminster, 1977).

3. C. Talbert, ed., *Reimarus: Fragments* (Philadelphia: For
tress, 1974).

4. See: D. F. Strauss, *The Life of Jesus Critically Examine*
(London, 1846); *A New Life of Jesus* (London, 1865).

5. A. Schweitzer, *The Quest for the Historical Jesus* (Nev
York: Macmillan, 1961), pp. 137–68.

6. R. Bultmann, *Kerygma and Myth* (New York: Harper
Row, 1961); *Jesus Christ and Mythology* (New York
Scribner's, 1958).

7. See E. McKnight, *What is Form Criticism?* (Phila
delphia: Fortress, 1969) and R. Bultmann, *The History o
the Synoptic Problem* (New York: Harper & Row, 1963)

8. See R. Bultmann, *Jesus Christ and Mythology*, pp. 19–21
Kerygma and Myth, p. 10.

9. R. Bultmann, "The Historical Jesus and the Kerygmati
Christ," in C. Braaten and R. Harrisville, eds., *The Histori
cal Jesus and the Kerygmatic Christ* (Nashville: Abingdon
1964), pp. 15–42. N. Perrin, *The Promise of Bultman*
(Philadelphia: Lippincott, 1969).

10. See Perrin, pp. 22–36.

11. See: H. Jonas, *The Gnostic Religion* (Boston: Beaco
Press, 1963).

12. M. Goulder, "Jesus, the Man of Universal Destiny," i
The Myth of God Incarnate, p. 49.

13. F. Young, "Two Roots of a Tangled Mass," in *Th*
Myth of God Incarnate, pp. 117–18.

14. Shortly after the publication of this work, several En
glish theologians published their answer in *The Truth o*
God Incarnate, ed. M. Green (London: Hodder an
Stoughton, 1977). Unfortunately the response is lacking i
serious scholarship.

5. For a good introduction to Bultmann the believer, see *Jesus and the Word* (New York: Scribner's, 1958).

5. For an overview of this controversy, see J. F. O'Grady, *Jesus, Lord and Christ,* Chapter 2. An extensive bibliography on the subject is also contained in this work.

4

JESUS THE
ETHICAL LIBERATOR

EACH SUNDAY a group of Christians gathered to celebrate the liturgy of the Eucharist in a poor village in Nicaragua. Instead of a homily, there was a dialogue after all listened to the Word of God. This Sunday the people had listened to Matthew 11:1–11—the story of the messengers sent by John the Baptist to Jesus. One of the listeners responded, "I said that it was also possible that John, in a deep depression in his prison, might be doubting that Jesus was the liberator."[1]

To someone suffering the oppression of economic, social and political control, Jesus stands for the one who brings freedom. He is the liberator.

Later in the discussion someone objected that Jesus was concerned about freedom from sin and not physical freedom. Another replied:

Freedom from sin and physical freedom are the same thing. To keep ourselves in poverty is a physical slavery, right? And it's sin too. Then what's the difference between physical freedom and freedom from sin? Sin is physical too, and to save ourselves we also need physical things.[2]

From the Archipelago Solentiname in Nicaragua to the Black theology in the United States, in all of the Third World countries and for any group that is suffering oppression, Jesus has taken on a new image. Th model is not mythological, nor does it focus on the Sec ond Person of the Blessed Trinity: rather, Jesus is th liberator of the oppressed. The mission of Jesus today i a political task. To understand the origin and meanin of this new model for Jesus demands an appreciation o the scriptural studies on Jesus the revolutionary, bu more importantly, it requires a deep study of and con cern for oppressed peoples.

Latin American theologians in particular have devel oped a Christology that provides a basis for the concer about liberation.[3] In the past, when liberation theolog was discussed, it was often dismissed as a passing fac based more upon economic need and political pressur than upon any sure foundation in Christian traditior With the publication of several books on theology b Latin American theologians, however, the movemen took on a different hue. Still, critics claimed that th movement lacked any clear Christology. This objectio was answered with the publication of works on Chris tology.[4] Now the movement has been established o sound scholarship presented in a way that must forc any systematic theologian to pay attention.

The liberation theologians base their theology on th historical Jesus. Juan Sobrino states that two reasons ex plain the current consensus among Latin America theologians: "First of all there is a clearly noticeable re semblance between the situation here in Latin Americ and that in which Jesus lived."[5] He does not claim tha there is an anachronistic resemblance, but that in Lati America, as opposed to other historical situations, th present condition is acutely felt and understood as a sin ful condition.

His second observation concerns the meaning of the ology and the origins of Christology: "They [the firs Christian communities] did not possess a fabricate Christology."[6] The theology developed around tw poles: the historical Jesus and the concrete situation o each community. The resurrection made faith possible, but in the development of a Christology based upon the resurrection the early Christians had to deal with the features of the life of Jesus and thus had to select those features which would best suit their concrete historical situation.

Today's Church faces the same prospect. Those who see Jesus as an ethical liberator compare the present situation in Latin America, or among any oppressed people, with the historical situation of Jesus. By means of this comparison, they seek to express in the most powerful way the faith that is present in the community. In the history of Christianity, each community has to make efforts to discover for itself the universal significance of Christianity that ultimately found its expression in Church dogma. Such an effort moves back and forth between the historical Jesus and what happened to him in his situation and what this same Jesus can mean to us in our situation. To return to the historical Jesus demands an understanding of his personal situation as a Jew with two millennia of Jewish tradition, as well as requiring an appreciation of him as the incarnate Word of God.

Christianity is heir to God's act of liberating the Jewish people from slavery. This figures prominently in the contemporary theology of liberation. The cry of "Let my people go" in Exodus 5:1 is echoed in many lands where oppression and faith are yoked together. Just as God once liberated the Jewish people from oppression, so he will continue to grant freedom to those who experience a similar oppression. This part of the Christian heritage forms a part of the actual historical background of Jesus. The second element of the double action on which Christianity is based is the struggle of Jesus himself. Condemned by the mighty of his day, he sufficiently impressed himself and his teachings on his followers so that, eventually, aided by the Spirit, they became the heralds of a new way of living.

Jesus as a historical person embodied the sense of freedom and love and created a new way of life. The first action, which was experienced by the Jews, under lies the historical roots of Christianity; the second reveals the radical consequences of this initial experience of the liberating God. The first action is easy enough to understand. People were oppressed socially, politically and economically and they were released from their bondage through the leadership of Moses. They began a new way of living that brought them a sense of personal and corporate freedom. While there are exegetical problems in understanding the meaning of "Let my people go" in the sense of personal freedom, there is no doubt that the end result was a sense of freedom and liberation, with the possibility of this new people deciding for themselves their personal and corporate destiny. This can be grasped more readily than the meaning of the liberation that Jesus himself accomplished as this is described in the New Testament.

THE KINGDOM OF GOD

THE KINGDOM of God as presented in the New Testament might best be considered a revolution of the old order. Jesus presented it as good news for the poor, light for the blind, hearing for the deaf, freedom for those in prison, liberation for the oppressed, pardon for sinners and life for the dead (Lk. 4:18–21; Mt. 11:3–5). This kingdom is not reserved for an afterlife, but involves an effort to transform the present world. Jesus offered a sense of liberation from all that was troubling people in human history: hunger, pain, injustice, suffering, oppression and death—a liberation that would affect not only the human race but the rest of creation as well (Rom. 8:22–23). Jesus as the liberator clearly stated that this hope was not some false utopia, but the actual experience of happiness for all. When Jesus began to preach he proclaimed, "The time

as come and the kingdom of God is at hand. Repent
nd believe the good news [Mk. 1:4]."

The expectation of a liberator was part of the specific
)ld Testament message as well as the hope of all hearts.
he Jews were led from the land of slavery into a
romised land, a land of milk and honey (Is. 65:17,
6:22). Isaiah looked forward to the time when all evil
nd conflict would be destroyed and all creation would
e at peace. The lion would lie down with the lamb
Is. 11:6). Paul, following Jesus, had a similar hope
n his vision of a time when God would be all in all
1 Cor. 15:28).

As the liberator, Jesus inaugurated this kingdom not
s an evolution of the present order but as an actual
evolution in the structures of this world. Jesus did not
imself create this new world, but he so liberated his
ollowers internally and so strongly encouraged them
hat they themselves would share in the revolution of
he social order. The new world will be restructured so
hat it can reveal the glory of God as experienced by
)eople, especially by those who have undergone cul-
ural, political, social or economic oppression. This
<ingdom is not just a future reality, but the presence of
he future, now.

To understand the intention of Jesus and his attitude
:oward the kingdom, we must see him as one who
would not regionalize the kingdom of God and limit it
:o one model. In his lifetime there were those who
wished to make him king, thus regionalizing the kingdom to one ideology and one political system. Jesus refused such a limitation. He battled against the current
structures, as can be seen in his quarrels with the Pharisees, but he rejected the aspirations for power of his
apostles. If he had done otherwise, he would have been
attempting to impose norms or solutions that would
have precluded other possible norms and solutions.
Jesus concerned himself with a form of liberation for
people that would allow them the opportunity to de-

velop a social order corresponding to the good news he
preached. People themselves would be able to translate
and make effective the teaching of Jesus in any time
and in any place. His openness to many possibilities and
his refusal to allow the society of his time to restrict the
kingdom of God ultimately led to his death. He was disturbing the established order. He would not allow the
Jewish interpretation of religion to be maintained as an
absolute. His accomplishment was to create a new attitude toward God, human life and the future and thus
inaugurate a new praxis which would anticipate the new
order for which all peoples hoped.

The spirit that Jesus manifested as a liberator was
born of a religious motivation, not a humanitarian one.
He was aware of his personal relationship to God and
sought to bring people into the same free and loving
relationship. His understanding of the meaning of God
and religion meant being involved in the affairs of people; thus what he proclaimed was not divorced from
their ordinary experience. The goodness of God included a sense of personal freedom as well as of social
freedom. Structures in both civil and religious society
were meant to manifest this freedom and not deny its
existence.

The kingdom of God signified all of this. It began in
Jesus, but it was not completed, since the liberator en-
trusted his followers to the task of establishing those
structures that best fulfill the sense of his preaching. He
gave the direction and people must make a response,
continuing the building of the kingdom that Jesus began
in preaching. The parable of the yeast (Mt. 13:33), of
the seed placed in the earth (Mt. 4:26–29), of the
wheat and the tares (Mt. 13:24–30), and the dragnet
of good and bad fish (Mt. 13:47–50) all speak of a
future which is nevertheless actual in the present. There
is not a complete break between the present and the future; rather, there exists a process of liberation which
involves the future's breaking into the present. Such at-

itudes will guard against making Christianity and its
ounder into some plastic image, since they ensure the
perspective of the historical liberating power of the
Lord.

The totality of salvation that is present in the risen
Lord does not excuse the faithful from working for the
experience of this salvation in a human way. There is a
relationship between the kingdom of God and the kingdom which is on earth; faith does not proclaim a flight
from the present world, but a renovation of this world.
Certainly we are now conscious that the field on which
the struggle is taking place is composed of forces of evil
as well as of good, but in this struggle we are involved
with more than "religious" questions. We are concerned
with political activity.

JESUS THE NONCONFORMIST

THE GOSPELS indicate that one of the characteristics of
Jesus was nonconformity.[7] He was a sign of contradiction (Lk. 2:34), pointing to a crisis in Judaism
(Jn. 7:43; 9:16; 10:19). He was not afraid to counteract the senseless casuistry of the purification rites
(Mk. 2:27) nor the matrimonial legislation (Mk.
10:11–12), nor the use or abuse of power (Lk.
22:25–28). He examined the entire law and the prophets and submitted everything to the criteria of love of
God and neighbor.[8] He liberated people not just in
theory but in practice, and dealt with those who were
oppressed by the system: women, children, tax collectors, public sinners, the afflicted in body and mind.
Jesus openly took their side and was identified not with
the establishment and the ruling class but with the
outcasts, the despised, the marginal people. What he
offered them was not a false sense of hope, but an attitude of mind that freed them from the oppression with
which they had been unjustly burdened.

When people were scandalized with his liberating

stance toward outcasts, he spoke the parable of the prodigal son (Lk. 15) or told them he was sent not to call the just but the unjust (Mt. 9:13). For Jesus the liberator there were no class distinctions: he welcomed prostitutes and heretics (Samaritans); he had a close relationship with Levi, a collaborator with the Romans (Mk. 2:15–17), with a Zealot (Mk. 3:18–19) and even with people who aspired to use power for their own advantage (Lk. 9:46). He broke down the barriers and liberated people in their social relationships by ignoring traditional social distinctions. His own attitude demonstrated his sense of personal freedom. He not only had the courage to preach liberation and freedom, but actually lived what he professed.[9] This alone would have caused great problems for the leaders of Jewish and Roman society.

UNIVERSAL VERSUS PARTICULAR

IN THE past, theologians and preachers proclaimed Jesus as universal savior. His life affected humanity; salvation meant a sense of peace, harmony and reconciliation that involved the entire universe. Jesus brought liberation from death and sin and suffering. Theologians used these terms and then spoke of liberation from the painful elements that are part of the human condition—but such a proclamation made sin and death and suffering universal categories divorced from their historical reality. If we accept this approach to Jesus, then it is difficult to understand why the powerful of his day condemned him. Jesus announced the good news by appropriating the words of Isaiah: "He has sent me to proclaim release for the captives, recovery of sight for the blind, to let the broken victims go free [Lk. 4:18]."

Jesus would not be content with a vague and general accommodation. He did not remain neutral with regard to the inherent contradictions of the society of his day; he actually took sides in the controversies. At the same

ime, he did not assume power, and thus disappointed
he Zealots.[10] He alienated people, since he attacked the
Pharisees and what they considered traditional religion,
and shocked the priests by rejecting their position of authority and privilege. Jesus' liberation of people was
more than just a spiritual liberation. He attempted to
release individuals from restraints here on earth so that
they could be free before God. Liberation was particular as well as universal. Jesus refused to preach a sense
of freedom that was divorced from historical reality. To
be truly liberated meant freedom from all oppression—
not in some general way, but in concrete historical circumstances of an individual's life. People do not live
abstract, universal lives, and so the freedom that Jesus
offered would not take refuge in false hopes. Liberation
was for the individual and it was particular.

POLITICAL VERSUS SPIRITUAL

JESUS as a liberator refused to assume power or to use
force or violence to transform his society. We do not
encounter a political messiah in the gospels, because
Jesus rejected this possibility. When the crowds wished
to make him king, he fled (Jn. 6:15). At the same
time, we would misrepresent the meaning of Jesus if we
attempted a purely spiritualistic interpretation of his
ministry. Jesus saw the kingdom of God in conflict with
the powers in this world and would not run away from
the battle. Nor can we think of the kingdom only as an
eschatological reality. The resurrection of Jesus did not
mean that the struggle for liberation was over, nor did
it mean that the promise of freedom was reserved for
the end of time. Easter was a sign of hope and an experience of freedom, but one which included struggle.

Jesus as the liberator struggled against the powerful
in favor of the oppressed, but he also frustrated some of
the oppressed. The Zealots of the time sought to discover in Jesus the leader who would guide them in

banishing the Roman occupation and who would rees
tablish Israel as a significant political force. The ver
disciples of the Lord seemed to share this viewpoint
even after the resurrection (Acts 1:16), but Jesu
would neither accept the role of a political messiah dur
ing his ministry nor after his resurrection.

This political refusal, however, should also be seen a
a political act. As messiah, he refused to change th
societal relationships by freeing people from being sub
ject to a powerful minority. Such a decision was politi
cally active, since Jesus as liberator gave to the peopl
the right to determine for themselves their own history
and society. Social relationships are never just natura
facts which Jesus could reestablish after they had been
abused or denied for a period of time; social rela
tionships are historical, and it is in producing socia
relationships based on justice, according to the needs o
the times, that people demonstrate that they can tak
the demands of the kingdom and the good news o
Jesus seriously in their own moment in history. Jesus i
the liberator since he recognizes that in politics peopl
can develop their social relationships according to th
prophetic demands whose champion the messiah had
become. The proclamation of the kingdom makes mor
evident the historical struggle that is necessary if peopl
are to be truly liberated.

To fail to see Jesus as ethical liberator causes som
Christians to retreat into a spiritual skepticism. History
and the struggle of peoples is real. The necessary reso
lution of social relationships demands a commitment to
the order that will bring this about. The Thessalonian
who waited for the heavens to open to reveal the com
ing of the Son of Man in power and majesty, and mean
while lived as parasites, have counterparts throughou
the history of Christianity. Some spiritual writers may
turn to the death and resurrection of Jesus as the once
for-all victory and on this basis put up with any injus
tice. But this denies the reality of Jesus as the one who

liberated people in more than just a spiritual sense. The tension between the spiritual aspect of the kingdom and the physical, material dimension that is so necessary for human life will remain. No theologian can retreat to the domain of the spirit in an exclusive sense and still be faithful to the teaching of Jesus.

THE PRESENT VERSUS THE FUTURE

JESUS did not offer any blueprint for the structures in society that would be necessary to usher in the kingdom. He did not advocate the overthrow of the contemporary political regime. Jesus accepted the present situation, but not in the sense of passive acquiescence; his followers were told to develop for themselves the structures in society that would encourage human development and thus hasten the final coming of the kingdom of God. The absolute presence of God in Jesus did not annihilate human history, since it is only there that our futures are made. In the preaching of God's reign by Jesus we can find the meaning for living with the present reality as we continue the earthly struggle for the future in which social relationships and social structures will be based upon the good news of the gospel. Jesus as liberator frees people from the past, not by creating a new present nor by destroying the present, but by allowing and encouraging people to create for themselves the future they desire. Jesus opens people up to their own future.[11]

In the Old Testament God took sides with the oppressed and led them to a new future. The exploited became the liberated as they moved out from under the yoke of social, political and economic control to set a destiny for themselves as free persons. God did not establish for them the social structures in which they would find their freedom, but gave them the impetus to work toward a better future.

In the New Testament we can also say that God took

sides in Jesus, but as was true in the Old Testamen
Jesus did not relieve humanity from the task of creatin
its own history and its own social order so that all peo
ple could stand in his presence in freedom. In Jesus th
goodness of salvation encouraged and impelled peopl
to create a social order which would correspond to th
injunction to feed the hungry, clothe the naked an
shelter the homeless. If the kingdom of God was to be
come a reality on earth, then exploitation must b
abolished. Since Jesus liberated people, those who hav
been freed must experience the liberation of the socia
order as well. "Sin is physical too, and to save ourselve
we also need physical things."[12] Salvation does no
mean some vague sense of feeling good or some spiri
tual "high." Salvation consists in the realistic awarenes
that the future is created in the present. There is n
freedom for anyone unless all are liberated from ever
oppression.

TACTICS

JESUS as a liberator did not offer a panacea or an unre
alistic utopia. We face a continual historical struggle i
which temporary solutions may be all that can be ex
pected at any one moment. But the failure to achiev
total liberation need not cause the movement to disinte
grate into a spiritual opiate. Tactics are necessary to de
stroy false bonds. Actual accomplishments of liberatio
are essential if there is to be present the hope of tha
full liberation which will be accomplished only at th
end of time. The presence of the spirit of Jesus deliver
his followers from any mythical character of liberation
since it makes the reality present, even if only in ar
inchoate way. With such an understanding of liberation
various tactics may be accepted as necessary—eve
those presented in Marxist categories. If there are n
such tactics then Christianity remains but an ineffectua

:ry, leading to resignation or to the rejection of Christianity itself.

This overview of Jesus as liberator[13] sets the scene for a further development that will involve a hermeneutical quest. The true theologian cannot be satisfied with an exegetical enterprise that remains self-enclosed, without concrete application.[14] We have already noted that the theology of Latin America comes out of praxis. The same is true for the Black theology of the United States. It is the experience of oppression over the past several hundred years that has formed the matrix for Christian thought, an experience of human suffering not unlike that experienced at the time of Jesus, as these theologians understand the gospel.

Former Christologies turned to the Scriptures and read the images of Jesus found therein in the light of his words and deeds and within the apocalyptic framework and sociological and cultural background of the times. Such an approach is not an end in itself, but must be joined to the hermeneutical approach that seeks the meaning that Jesus conveyed or what some will call the *ipsissima intentio Jesu,* just as more traditional theologians refer to *ipsissima verba Jesu.*[15] This hermeneutic is discovered in the words and deeds of Jesus, but must be carefully sifted out on the basis of an appreciation of his experience as well as of the experience of the one who actually does the sifting.

To know the meaning of the kingdom of God in Judaism and to Jesus himself is insufficient; to discover the meaning of the blessedness that is given to the poor in relationship to the words of Jesus is equally unacceptable. Rather, we must ask what is the meaning of the kingdom of God at its deepest level and how this influences and affects the continual quest for its presence. We must seek out the apocalyptic message of Jesus and not be content to say that it involves the coming of the Son of Man in glory, the resurrection of the dead and the inauguration of the new heaven and earth.

What must be asked is: What is the message of th
apocalyptic imagery of Jesus? For the theologians
liberation, the kingdom of God and the apocalypti
message of Jesus find expression in the theology tha
they have experienced in the suffering of oppresse
groups. There is a difference in time and space and lar
guage, but careful analysis shows this new image
Jesus as liberator to be the expression of the heart
the Christian message. The kingdom of God is a tota
structural revolution.

Faith proclaims this kingdom to be the hope of a
generations, but the gospel does not espouse any partic
ular means to achieve it. No definite program is ad
vocated; what we have is an attitude based upon the in
tention of Jesus as seen in the gospels. If Christian
decide to take power because this tactic appears at th
present time to be the only alternative to continuous op
pression, it is done not in a spirit of vengeance, but as
reconciling response to a particular problem of socia
structures. If other Christians at another time renounc
power and preach nonviolence as the only tactic accept
able, this too can be the expression of a decision in ac
cord with the intention of Jesus. Liberation is related t
the kingdom of God and the preaching of Jesus, bu
cannot simply be identified with that kingdom in th
gospel. The kingdom, after all, is the presence of Go
in a total and complete way which encompasses the en
tirety of creation. On the other hand, it is also true tha
anything that can prepare the social order for the pres
ence of God, so that God can be all in all, is not only
possibility for the Christian, but an imperative.

Faith gives us the assurance and guarantee that th
future of the human race is the full liberation by Jesu
that has taken place in the resurrection, but it does no
give us the key to solve all of the political, economic
and social problems that we face as Christians. Chris
tianity is not an ideology and thus does not have a se
pattern to impose upon the social order. Nor can we say

that one approach is valid for all times and places and people. (Rather, the presence of the liberating spirit of Jesus gives the believer the opportunity to judge wisely the signs of the times and seek those tactics that will be effective in bringing some of the social structures into conformity with the gospel. Jesus desires believers to be creative and imaginative through the analysis of the present scene and in the service of a liberating ideal.) The Christian should never fear to make a definite decision and risk failure in an effort to continue the mission of the Lord. For this we pray daily, "Thy kingdom come." What will be the concrete shape of the Christian response cannot be predetermined. The believer attends to the call of the situation and seeks any expression in which the eschatological kingdom can be made manifest in this moment of time so that people actually experience something of the freedom that Jesus himself promised to all his followers. Jesus was the liberator and continues to effect what he once preached through the activities of his present-day followers.

TRANSFORMATION THROUGH SUFFERING

TRUE transformation takes place on every level: the political, social, economic and cultural. The kingdom is present where there is a victory of justice over injustice, the defeat of oppression and the establishment of a wider sense of freedom. Thus no believer can neglect the present for the sake of some future experience of salvation. Any struggle toward freedom from economic, political or social oppression is not merely a political imperative, it is an imperative based upon an understanding of Jesus as the true liberating force in human history. Faith impels working for the transformation of structures. The actual quest for the liberation of all people will also involve suffering. The cross of the liberator is not far from the backs of those who are trying to maintain their faith and continue this liberating force in the world today. Oppression by the ruling class, imprisonment, torture and even death were the experience of the liberating Lord. His followers will experience the same in their efforts to accomplish the vision that he offered.

The Christian theologians of Latin America as well as the Black theologians of the United States and, increasingly, the theologians of Third World countries in general, see in the model of the ethical liberator a powerful response to questions that plague their societies. They also recognize that such a model allows them to move beyond the Western European type of theology that has characterized much of Christian theology for centuries. The advantages of such a model will prove important for many future generations of theologians, as well as for Church leaders.

First of all, this model corresponds to a felt need in developing countries and among the oppressed in any society. Some claim that the traditional Jesus stands for death in Latin America and that "Che" Guevara represents life and destiny.[16] The model of Jesus as ethical liberator offers to Latin American Christians a sense of Jesus that counteracts this false image. Christianity becomes not an ancient artifact, but a reality that is concerned with the problems of everyday life. Jesus is part of the struggle that people experience; he gives not only the encouragement but the impetus to overcome this oppression and strive for more just social structures.

Secondly, the model brings to the fore the sense of social justice that has long been part of the Christian message but has been all too frequently overlooked.[17] It is well and good for Popes to write encyclicals on social justice, but when Jesus himself is seen as a liberator, as one who destroys class distinctions, as one who actually strikes out against a prevailing social order, then it is easier for believers who subscribe to such a doctrine of social justice to use the image of Jesus as a powerful means of convincing their fellow believers and religious aders who are not yet awakened to the demands of social justice.

Thirdly, the model speaks not just to those who are experiencing oppression on an economic and political front, but to anyone who is seeking a sense of personal freedom from the oppression that modern society, whether capitalist or socialist, imposes on its members. Jesus is not a weak-willed messiah, but a strong man of deep conviction who allows people of all persuasions the opportunity to throw off the shackles that have kept them in darkness for centuries. He calls them to rejoice in the sunlight of freedom.

Fourthly, the model speaks to the actual structure of the Church and its self-understanding. If Jesus is the liberator, then the Church cannot function in theory or practice as an institution that contributes to oppression, whether in social, moral or dogmatic matters. If people are freed from unjust restraint, then the Church itself cannot impose such restraints. The believer has been liberated and should feel liberated in the community of faith.

Liberation theology involves more than just Latin America, underdeveloped nations and the American Black.[18] Any group that has been victimized has a right to be liberated and to experience the freedom of God. Any group that has been oppressed should feel that the Church, both in theory and practice, is on its side, whether that group is composed of Third World people or the Black community in the United States or women throughout the world or the gay community or children or the aged. The Church that upholds Jesus as a liberator of all people must seek positive ways to offer the sense of that liberation to anyone, any group that has been unjustly denied a rightful position in society. If Christology is the foundation for an ecclesiology, this model has much to say to the understanding of the Church as well as Church practice. The advantages are overwhelming, as are the implications.

Finally, this model has implications not just for eccle
siology, but for all of theology. Jesus as the liberato
will affect social theology and the whole question o
Christian morality. Too often in the past morality wa
identified with sexual morality, and even in that are:
there was often more oppression than liberation. Mo
rality is also involved with the social dimension o
human life, and social theology will be the result of th
interaction of the concrete need for liberation and th
traditional understanding of Christian theology. If th
Church is also a liberator, it cannot impose sanctions o
thinkers just because their conclusions are not clearly i
accord with traditional theology. Freedom to think an
express an opinion, even publicly, must be part of th
liberation that Jesus offers. Otherwise the liberator i
concerned with the false bondage of the human body
but is uninterested in the equally false bondage of th
human spirit. Jesus of Nazareth was concerned wit
every aspect of the human person that might experienc
oppression and bondage.

While the advantages of this model are as exciting a
its many possible applications, there are also some no
table drawbacks. These, however, should not vitiate th
positive effect of this model of Jesus on contemporar
theology.

The liberation theologians tend to make Jesus a revo
lutionary and to lose sight of the Christian belief tha
has seen him as the Son of God. As they emphasize th
liberator, the concern that the oppressed be freed i
every way can diminish appreciation of the divine ele
ment in Jesus of Nazareth. He becomes an earlie
"Che" Guevara, rather than the Son of God who ex
pressed in his life the presence of the divine, even in th
midst of unjust social conditions.

Secondly, the model tends to be reductionist. A fu
ture seen exclusively in social and economic term
shortchanges the true future, which, within any socia
and political system, also involves the religious and th

ultural, and includes the interactions of diverse peoples
rom diverse viewpoints and ways of life. The world has
rown too complex to be viewed totally in terms of eco-
omics and social reform. The interplay of many disparate elements that will never be completely reconciled
must coexist within a creative tension.

Thirdly, the tactics endorsed by liberation theology
an be misunderstood. Because Jesus used violence in
he temple does not mean that the Christian must turn
o violence in the name of Jesus to overthrow an unjust
ystem. Even nonviolence can in itself be a form of vio-
ence. How must a believer decide what tactics are to be
used in trying to fulfill the destiny that Jesus has offered
us? So many other considerations must be weighed to
ensure that the good outweighs the evil in any course of
ction. This is particularly true when Christians become
involved with a Marxist approach to life. Marxist tac-
ics can be accommodated to the Christian gospel, but
he extent of that accommodation is limited, particu-
arly because the Marxist system, as we know it, at-
empts to exclude any sense of the presence of the divine. Humanism is not the same as Christianity.

Fourthly, the model of Jesus as liberator does not
deal sufficiently with the power of evil in the world and
in every individual. The kingdom of God will not be realized as a result of human efforts alone. We are engaged in a struggle that will be resolved not through
human power, but through the intervention of the divine, just as that kingdom was inaugurated by the intervention of the divine. The future—the harmony and
peace promised by the gospel and by the liberation
theologians—is not just around the corner, precisely because of the existence of evil. Liberation theologians
may appeal to those who seek power to do so in a con-
rolled way. Unfortunately, those who seek and actually
seize power are subject to the same temptation to abuse
t as those from whom they took it in the first place.

Finally, the chief weakness of the concept of Jesus as

the liberator lies in the inability to describe "liberation
empirically. What does it mean to be liberated? Ho
can we move from the level of rhetoric and swee
sounding words to the level of everyday living? Doe
this mean that all the wealth of the world is to be redis
tributed so that everyone has the same amount withou
any distinctions? How would this affect the creative a:
pect of the human spirit? Does liberation mean tha
rules and regulations, especially within the Churcl
have no place? How can liberation be practically expe
rienced by an Indian in Latin America, or by a corpc
rate executive in New York controlled by the demand
of his multinational conglomerate? How would libera
tion, as defined by such theologians, be a guarantee of
better social order?

Certainly the New Testament gives impetus to th
model of Jesus as ethical liberator; it also offers to cor
temporary Christianity some correctives to its socia
doctrine that long have been overlooked and even a
times have been rejected. The contribution of liberatio
theologians who deal with the historical Jesus and at th
same time seek to relate this Jesus to the needs of ou
own times can never be banished to the backwaters c
theology. For too long theology has been hampered b
the limitations of European philosophy without thos
limitations being recognized. Now we have an indepen
dent movement that has arisen out of need and that cor
responds to the best of the Christian theological tradi
tion. The interplay of the various theological a
proaches may be the only hope that theology has c
making contribution to a world content to ignore it
reflections.

At the same time it would be highly dangerous t
erect this model into the new paradigm that will seek t
respond to the various questions troubling not only th
Christian Church but human society itself. We live in
very complex world that cannot function without the in
teraction of many disparate, belligerent and even essen

ally contradictory groups. Theology cannot afford to
e so unrealistic as to offer solutions that fail to take
nto account the complexities of life in a day when a
ecision made in a small Arab state or a Black nation
an set off tremors throughout the world in a matter of
noments.

Liberation is part of the Christian experience because
: is part of the teaching of Jesus. That much cannot be
ainsaid. Liberation as *the* paradigm of Christology, as
he instrument that Christian theologians will use to re-
pond to the demands of the contemporary Church and
he contemporary world, is another matter. As in the
ase of the previous models, it has definite advantages
nd definite disadvantages. How can we understand the
neaning of the life and death and resurrection of Jesus
nd how can we apply this understanding to the needs
f today while at the same time preserving the insights
f two thousand years of Christian faith? Liberation
heology is part of the answer, but not the whole an-
wer.

NOTES

. See E. Cardenal, *The Gospel in Solentiname*, vol. II
Maryknoll: Orbis, 1978), p. 2.

. *Ibid.*, p. 4.

. See H. Assmann, *Theology for a Nomad Church*
Maryknoll: Orbis, 1976); G. Gutierrez, *A Theology of
iberation* (Maryknoll: Orbis, 1973); R. Alves, *A Theology
f Human Hope* (Washington: Corpus, 1969); J. Miranda,
eing and the Messiah (Maryknoll: Orbis, 1977); L. Boff,
Salvation in Christ and the Process of Liberation," *Con-
'ium*, vol. 96 (New York: Paulist, 1974); J. Segundo, *Lib-
ation Theology (Maryknoll: Orbis, 1975); G. Gutierrez
nd R. Shaull, *Liberation and Change* (Atlanta: John Knox,
977).

. See J. Sobrino, *Christology at the Crossroads* (Mary-
noll: Orbis, 1978); L. Boff, *Jesus Christ Liberator* (Mary-
noll: Orbis, 1978).

. Sobrino, p. 12.

6. *Ibid.*, p. 13.

7. J. Ernst, "Der Nonkonformisus Jesus," in *Anfang d* *Christologie* (Stuttgart, 1972), pp. 145–58. The nonco formist attitude is evident in a reading of the gospels. S also E. Kasemann, *Jesus Means Freedom* (Philadelphia Fortress, 1970).

8. Käsemann, Chapter 1.

9. *Ibid.*, p. 27. See also O'Grady, *Jesus, Lord and Chri* Chapter 1.

10. See M. Hengel, *Was Jesus a Revolutionary?* (Phil delphia: Fortress, 1971). This work contains an extensiv bibliography on works prior to 1970. See also O. Cullman *Jesus and the Revolutionaries* (New York: Harper & Ro 1975).

11. See C. Duquoc, "Liberation and Salvation in Jes Christ," in *Liberation Theology and the Message of Salv tion* (Pittsburgh: Pickwick, 1978), p. 53. This collection essays, mainly by European theologians, contains many va uable insights into the meaning of liberation theology.

12. Cardenal, p. 4.

13. See *Concilium*, vol. 2, #10 and vol. 6, #10. Both issu are devoted to the question of liberation theology. The co tributors are Latin Americans as well as Europeans.

14. See G. Montague, "Hermeneutics and the Teaching Scripture," *Catholic Biblical Quarterly*, vol. 41 (1979), p 1–17.

15. Boff, "Salvation in Christ and the Process of Liber tion," in *Concilium*, p. 80. The Latin of the first mean "The very intention of Jesus"; the second, "the very wor of Jesus."

16. G. Casalis, "Jésus de Nazareth, 'Che' Guevara et l Conquistadores." A shorter version is "Jésus, ni vaincu monarque céleste." *Témoignage Chrétien*, #1503, Ap 1973, pp. 17–18. Quoted in G. Casalis, "Liberation a Conscientization in Latin America," *Liberation Theolog and the Message of Salvation*, p. 114.

17. Paul VI, *Progressio Populorum* (New York: Pauli 1967).

18. This chapter has avoided separating the various o pressed groups and has tried to deal with general them that might be applied to all of the oppressed. For the trea ment of the Black liberation movement in the United State see the works of James Cone, especially *God of the O*

ressed (New York: Seabury, 1975) and *A Black Theology of Liberation* (Philadelphia: Lippincott, 1970). With regard to feminist theology, much of the contemporary literature, in the opinions of the authors themselves, has gone beyond Christianity. For the Christian perspective see: . Russell, *Human Liberation in a Feminist Perspective—a Theology* (Philadelphia: Westminster, 1974); R. Ruether, *Religion and Sexism* (New York: Simon & Schuster, 1974). The early Mary Daly writings, e.g. *The Church and the Second Sex* (New York: Harper & Row, 1968) are Christian. Her later works are professedly post-Christian. Almost nothing from the gay liberation movement can be termed Christian other than rebuttals of Church pronouncements condemning homosexuality and attempts at calling attention to the question.

The basic principles presented in this chapter should apply to all minority groups and to any oppressed person or peoples.

5

THE HUMAN FACE OF GOD

RECENT WORK ON the meaning of Christology has focused on the humanity of Jesus. The uniqueness and universality of the Lord is not his divinity but his humanity. Movement back and forth, from an emphasis on the humanity to an emphasis on the divinity, has characterized the history of theology. The ancient school of Antioch, which emphasized the humanity, and that of Alexandria, which emphasized the divinity, have had their counterparts throughout history. Today the pendulum seems to have swung in favor of Antioch.

Theologians present Jesus in the context of anthropology. He is the point toward which the human race has always been directed;[1] or, the humanity of Jesus is a new way of being human;[2] or the deity does not exclude but actually includes humanity;[3] or the human in Jesus is the realization of the divine.[4] These new approaches are found in popular magazines as well as in scholarly journals, so the Christian world knows what is being said, even if at times there is little understanding.

The principle that underlies this approach locates the unique universality in Jesus precisely in his being human. This Christology is not from above and deductive, but from below and inductive. Theologians do not discuss something that is above or below or beside, but a reality that is within; the human expresses the divine. God chose as revelation the human form, the man

Jesus. The mystery of Jesus lies in his humanity. Th human becomes the localization of the divine. With th perspective theologians must ask, "What does it mea to be human and what does it mean to be divine?"

THE PROBLEMATIC

AT FIRST sight it seems easy to respond to the questic "What does it mean to be human?" On closer scrutin the answer is not so evident. What characterizes humar ity? Is there a difference between being human as a ma and as a woman? Does age affect the meaning of hu manity? Do circumstances such as culture, educatior Are there limits to what a human being can be? Ca what is human be defined as "what humans do"? If s killing and destroying are as human as love and con passion.

What does it mean to be divine? Everyone has son idea of divinity: power, knowledge, eternity, authorit control, love, mercy—all have been associated with d vinity. But do we know what divinity means? If Gc has created us in his image, have we done little mo than repay the compliment? When we accept a divir revelation, how much of the content is the result c human projection, offering God-for-us but not God-ir himself? Does the unveiling of God imply a furthe veiling?

Christianity believes that Jesus revealed God. Br how is it possible for the human to be the vehic of the divine? Can we separate what is human ar divine in Jesus? If everything is perceived as bot human and divine, do we lose sight of the divinity, of the humanity? At the very outset we face a proble in trying to discover how the human can be the expre sion of the divine: we are not sufficiently clear on th meaning of humanity and surely cannot delineate th meaning of divinity.

The behavioral sciences in recent years have show

hat words like humanity, human nature and human be-
avior are empty formulas that can be filled with dis-
arate elements. Humans kill and betray; they lie and
ause suffering as well as love and forgive. The most
oble qualities can be predicated of being human, as
an the most debased.

Theologians tell us that the concepts of the divine
eed rethinking; God can be in process. This means
hat the qualities that we traditionally have associated
vith God can be forgotten. God can *become* in human
istory. Change is possible even with God—but have
ve here fallen into the same trap of creating God in our
wn image?

The ability to respond to all of the above questions
scapes our grasp. Yet, as Christians we have a faith
tatement that God is present in Jesus and we come to
now God through Jesus; he is the human face of
God.[5] "Philip, he who sees me sees the Father" (Jn.
4:9). Since theology is faith seeking understanding, we
an accept the faith statement and then go on to dis-
over some of the contents of that faith statement, even
f we are forever limited in our conclusions.

THE FOUNDATION

HE examination of Jesus as the human face of God in-
olves questions of anthropology as well as of history.
Vas Jesus, in a historical moment, the fullness of what
t means to be human, the definitive and eschatological
nan, the new man, the primordial image for all of hu-
nanity? Do we learn what it means to be human by ob-
erving the life and death of this historical person?
These questions presuppose another faith statement:
umankind is created in the image of God.

*So God created man in his own image, in the image
of God he created him; male and female he created
them. (Gen. 1:27)*

Within the Judaic-Christian heritage all people a
created in the image of God; they can manifest Go
every person can be the vice-regent of God, manifestir
some of the qualities of the divine. The image is n
limited to the spiritual nature of the person but involv
the totality. An inherent dignity results, which is ou
human heritage and destiny.[6]

Christians recognize Jesus to be the image of God i
an exemplary way:

> He is the image of the invisible God; the first born o
> all creation. (Col. 1:15)
> He reflects the glory of God, and bears the ver
> stamp of his nature. (Heb. 1:3)

But Jesus is not separated from others who are als
created in the image of God. He will always be th
firstborn of many brethren and like us in all things bu
sin (Heb. 4:15). Understanding Jesus as the huma
face of God depends upon first believing that every pe
son is created in the image of God and can thus reflec
the divine.

If we are to fill out the words "humanity" an
"human nature" with content and then apply them t
Jesus, however, we cannot just predicate our way o
being human as the final criterion for the humanity o
Jesus. There will be differences as well as similaritie
Jesus lived, for example, without the influence of ev
and sin. In faith we may learn that our understandin
of being human is not accurate. In Jesus of Nazaret
we learn a meaning of being human sufficiently tran
scendent to apply to every human being. Our humanit
or our idea of what it means to be human is not th
measure of evaluating Jesus, but rather his humanity i
the criterion by which we not only judge ourselves bu
even come to realize our potential.

Jesus as the human face of God was the revelation i
a personal way of the meaning of God. The two ele
ments, the human and the divine, are not disparate o

parated, but are united in one historical person. This
plies further consequences, for we must also admit
at the revelation of God took place in this personal
ay, circumscribed within the finite limits of the human
sus. In this historical person, we believe, we can expe-
ence the presence of a being at one and the same time
or humanity and for God."[7]

WHY JESUS WAS THE HUMAN FACE OF GOD

ALL people are created in the image of God, if all
ve the potential to manifest the divine, then why is
sus singled out to be the human face of God in an ex-
mplary way? What is it in Jesus that differentiates him
om millions of others who bear the face of the human
d contain the stamp of the divine? The human ex-
bits inherent limitations in attempting to express the
vine. We need not try to measure Jesus against some
ostract concept of humanity; we need not set out to es-
blish *a priori* principles upon which we can deduce
e reasons why Jesus is the exemplary image of God.
ather, we deal with the human Jesus and relate his ex-
erience to all human experiences. We study his life to
scover how, in his living, others experienced the di-
ne. By this means we will discover what humanity
eans, or at least we will uncover what humanity
eant to the historical Jesus as recorded by those who
elieved he was the presence of God.

Such an attempt involves investigating the self-
wareness of Jesus. That immediately causes hesitation.
low can we enter into the personality of Jesus, seeking
unravel the fundamental way in which Jesus is pres-
t to himself as an individual? The task of exploring
neself is difficult enough; how much more difficult it
ust be to attempt to deal with the self-awareness of
nother. Yet, the words, actions and attitudes of Jesus
s recorded in the gospels can teach us about his self-
nderstanding. The study must always be incomplete,

but with careful examination of the impact Jesus h[a]
upon others we can gain some entrance into his pe
sonal life. This helps us to situate Jesus in relationsh
to others and at the same time reveals his distincti·
personality.

JESUS' CONCEPT OF GOD

MANY major religions present an image of God as
loving parent, a Father. Judaism recognized the pate
nity of God, and it was in this atmosphere that Jes·
grew up. But Jesus was not content to affirm God as h
Father in the same way every other pious Jew wou
address God. For Jesus, God was *Abba*. God was lil
the loving parent who responds to a small child. The·
was an intimate relationship between God and Jes·
different from that of other people. Jesus always disti
guished this relationship. He spoke of my God and yo·
God, my Father and your Father, and never our F·
ther.[8] The universal meaning of Jesus contained in th
unique experience of God was at the very heart of h
message and ministry.

The study of the gospels also discloses a keen sen·
of dependency upon God. Everything Jesus has he h[a]
received from his Father; the Father has taught him al
has given him direction; he has been sent to accomplis
the mission of the Father; the Father is greater tha
Jesus and it is the Father's will that Jesus will accom
plish.[9] In all of religious experience the sense of depen
dence and creatureliness is significant.[10] The trace [c]
God present in human life is actually experienced b
some, even though it is denied by others. The awarene·
of limitations, of a lack of fulfillment in life, the sens
of mortality—all can contribute to an awakening of th
question of God. Do people live in isolation or in nee
of others? Can personal relations fulfill the need for
person to move out of himself or herself, or is there a
other force, a power, an ultimate person who can giv·

e true foundation for dependence and creatureliness?
Evidently for Jesus the sense of dependence and
creatureliness is related to his self-awareness of God in
s life as *Abba*. Jesus relates to God not with a sense
identity, since he will always maintain the difference
etween himself and his Father, but in the spirit of rev-
ation. He can reveal God as Father, as *Abba,* because
sus is God's Son. The union of willing and even of
eing makes Jesus present where God the Father is
resent and vice versa.

PERSONAL AWARENESS OF GOODNESS

VERYONE experiences moments in life of personal
orth and goodness. Jesus had a unique sense of his
oodness. He did not live a fragmented life; he pos-
essed a harmony that resulted in a consistency in all of
s words and actions. He maintained a tranquillity,
ven in the midst of the greatest conflicts, that caused
dmiration. Jesus was aware of his own principles and
ould not compromise them; he lived what he believed
 an integral way.

Everyone possesses an awareness of similar qualities,
ut with a difference. The power of evil and sin waxes
rong in the world and in the hearts of people. Instead
f contributing to a better environment, people tend to
ake the evil in the environment ever stronger, which
 turn makes the affirmation of this same evil easier by
ersonal sin.[11] Lives that are fragmented, out of har-
ony, lacking in consistency, filled with compromise in
e midst of personal turmoil, such lives have charac-
rized the history of the human race. Jesus lived
ifferently.

He did not repay evil with evil; he did not treat peo-
le in kind. Jesus decided how he would live his life
nd would not brook any interference. Jesus did not re-
liate against the people who maltreated him. The envi-
onment was evil, but instead of contributing to the

strength of the evil, he lessened its power by his mai
festation of goodness, which absorbed the evil ai
transformed it. He lived as the compassionate, kind ai
forgiving friend, even when he was offered rejectio
cynicism and resentment. He knew his God, knew I
mission and lived accordingly. His life was remarkab
because of his ability to express the power of goodnes

INTERNAL VERSUS EXTERNAL

THE GOODNESS that people express has to be viewed
relationship to the evil that also exists in the huma
heart. A lack of consistency characterizes both o
inner human spirit and our external actions. Paul reco
nized this tension when he wrote:

For I do not do the good that I want, but the ei
that I do not want, is what I do. (Rom. 7:19)

When faced with goodness, people often react again
it. They respond with resentment, or attempt to belitt
or deny. When faced with evil, people often accept i
even though they know that evil is to be resisted. Tl
war of the members against the spirit is fought on tl
plains of the human heart, with frequent casualties.

Jesus seems not to have experienced this intern
warfare. What he did was surely learned from his env
ronment, but what was appropriated was the goodne
and what was rejected was the evil. His actions, h
words, even his basic attitude toward human li
seemed to have its roots within. Jesus lived by transfe
ring the epicenter of his life to God, to *Abba,* and th
the externals always expressed the internal principl
This does not mean that he found his center of exi
tence outside of himself; rather he discovered his cent
was his relationship to God and thus he could live
harmonious life in which the outward expression flowe
from an inner conviction. The closer a person is

God, the more freedom that person experiences. Jesus, the graced man, lived in freedom and in harmony.

VALUE AND PURPOSE

FINALLY, Jesus lived with a definite sense of purpose for his life and with an energy that defies imitation. He was too sure, too definite, too aware of his value and his mission to ever be compared with others. His presence in human history can have a definite effect on every person, especially when it comes to questions about the ultimate meaning of personal life or the meaning of God, for in Jesus we can all recognize the fusion of principle and practice. Jesus saw his purpose and meaning in light of his proclamation of the kingdom of God. He knew that no final response can be given to the quest for meaning unless it includes the presence of God and unless the communion that should exist between God and his people is personally accepted.

For Christians who struggle to discover personal meaning and the overall purpose of their lives, the unique universality of Jesus will always involve the two poles of his own meaning: his relationship to God and the way he expressed this relationship in his life.[12] To relate to God as *Abba*, the human would have to be elevated and somehow participate in the realm of the divine, otherwise the divinity would not become part of personal experience. No one could relate to God as Jesus did unless God invited such a relationship and created its possibility. All people are created in the image of God, and this abstract belief becomes concretized in the actual inclusion of the religious element in the human search for meaning. Anyone who seeks to discover some purpose in life must include the divine, precisely because God created all in his image. Jesus fulfilled this human destiny. He lived for God and all who met him knew it.

Comparisons can certainly be made to other human beings who lived with a sense of dependence, found purpose in the divine or spiritual dimension and expressed some goodness in life, but the life of Jesus is more than just the sum total of the best of human qualities that have been expressed in history. He founded his life on his self-awareness and his sense of God. He appears to be the man without sin, able to live in the human and sinful environment without feeling its sting and without affirming its presence by personal ratification. His sense of purpose, his mission, is inscribed within and not just from without. Nor did he seem to struggle, as we must, to achieve tranquillity and harmony. The level of humanity he reached is the goal that all people seek; he remains, even in his unique universality, the firstborn of many brethren.

If "humanity" or "human nature" can be empty formulas that need to be filled with content, the life of Jesus gives the elements that will make up the content of the human in its highest form. If the divine can be expressed to human beings only in a human way, then the highest example of the human spirit can alone be the vehicle that God uses to reveal himself.

When we combine the human and the divine and speak of Jesus as the human face of God, we still are involved in a faith statement, but one that has been unfolded. We have some idea why Jesus was the human face of God in an eminent way and can still relate him to the universal human potential of being the image of God. Once we have dealt with why Jesus could be the expression of God in this preeminent way, the question still remains: "How was Jesus the human face of God?"

HOW JESUS REVEALED THE FATHER

IT IS clear from the gospels how contingent, ambivalent, limited and precarious the human life of Jesus was. He lived as a man, not as a woman and not as androgynous. He lived in Palestine under Roman occupation, with all of the contingencies and limitations that such a narrow mode of existence imposed. He did not benefit from world culture or world knowledge; he did not act and react with people of vastly divergent backgrounds and experiences. He lived an ordinary life in his own historical setting.

The evangelists do not present a biography of Jesus in any sense, but in their writings we can discover some aspects of his personality and life that we often overlook and which are important if we try to understand him as the human face of God. He slept, ate and drank, went to parties, enjoyed the company of friends, was part of a family, lived in a small community; he wept over the failure of people to listen to him, felt frustrated with his disciples, grew angry and disappointed. These aspects of his life manifest his humanity and surely do not demonstrate any great originality.[13] He lived as part of Roman-dominated Palestine in an eclectic environment, comprised of many philosophical systems and religious strains. In this world of contrasts Jesus stood out, however, as a remarkable person. He caused his listeners to wonder, to be shocked, to be scandalized. At one point even his own family thought he was out of his mind (Mk. 3:21). The evangelists are aware of his uniqueness, but do not deliberately contrast him with his contemporaries. He seems quite ordinary most of the time. He lived a hidden life for many years, became an itinerant preacher for a brief period and finally was crucified. Yet, when these same writers treat of his power and his influence over people, they show him displaying a quality that far exceeds ordinary human expression. Jesus possessed a transcendence, but one that made itself felt in and through the ordinary.

Both the ordinary and extraordinary are evident in the gospels, but the ordinary aspects of life—his rela-

tionships with people, his attitude toward Judaism, h
sense of forgiveness, his sensitivity toward others, h
openness to people's problems, his delight in huma
friendships, his pain at the lack of understanding of h
disciples, his frustration with the hardness of people
hearts—bear the expression of the divine. As th
human face of God, every detail in his life shared i
this transcendence. We should not be concerned wit
isolating moments of the life of the Lord, but with th
manifestations of the divine that shone through the o1
dinary elements of his human life.

The attitudes of Jesus figure significantly in unde1
standing how Jesus reflected God the Father. The hea1
of his gospel message is that God as Father is mindft
of humankind and cares for all. Jesus bore witness t
the indestructible certainty that God offers salvatior
This reflects a personal attitude, a conviction that salva
tion—the making whole of humanity and the perfectio
of the individual—is possible and that ultimately th
meaning in life involves the fullest expression of pe1
sonal freedom and liberation. Giving oneself to Go
paradoxically brings personal freedom. Jesus expresse
these attitudes in how he lived and also in how he died
In his attitude toward life he maintained a fruitful ten
sion between the contradictory poles of suffering, evi
and sin, and salvation linked with final and irrevocabl
good. In Jesus the goodness outweighed the evil tha
surrounded him; thus he could give others an exampl
of how to resist the evil and accept and manifest th
good. The basis for this attitude was the belief tha
God, *Abba,* is greater than all suffering and grief an
greater even than our ability to accept goodness. Cre
ation reflects the goodness of God. Such a positive atti
tude revealed Jesus' personal conviction of how Go
regarded humankind.

The attitudes displayed by Jesus in his personal con
cern for the poor, the compassion he offered to thos
who were the outcasts of society, the kindness he man

ifested to sinners, to widows, to children, to his disciples
and friends—all these are human dimensions of his personality, but they also express God's concerns. Jesus
possessed a universality that included the possibility of
the conquest of all personal and social forms of alienation. The sense of separateness, the experience of living
marginally, the isolation that causes so much pain can
be resolved into a harmonious and fruitful life. The
peace does not exist only on the interior plane, nor
should it be seen as simply a social phenomenon.
Rather, it is a combination of the two. Jesus did not retreat from the marketplace of human life, and thus his
meaning, his revelation of the healing of the torn fabric
of humanity, had to be accomplished in the domains of
both the personal and the social. His personal attitude
underlines the interrelationship of the two elements.
People will hurt personally in a way that no social or
political cure will be able to help, and vice versa. The
death of a mother or father inflicts pain personally, just
as subhuman housing, lack of education, restrictions on
travel and the inability to participate in the destiny of
one's country cause suffering socially and politically.
Jesus, in his attitude toward human problems and
human needs, offered a universal significance that
would respond to the various phases and facets of
human alienation. He preached and lived universal reconciliation.

Jesus revealed the meaning of God in his attitude
toward liberation, freedom and salvation. A feeling of
apartness or alienation often causes or contributes to
struggle in life, and so Jesus offered an attitude of creative love for all. Based upon the freedom given by
God and the salvation promised, Jesus believed that reconciliation was possible, and he actually lived according
to this principle. No one was excluded; no one need feel
left out. He welcomed into his company prostitutes,
widows, tax collectors, sinners. The communion that

Jesus preached was experienced in his person and offered to those who would respond to him in faith.

Jesus did not offer an absolute principle, but reminded people of a possibility that could be realized. Jesus gave to human history not the final answer to the question of the search for meaning and liberation, but rather the expectation that humanity can be liberated completely—not by seeking something outside of human history, but by seeking something within the human situation. Freedom and liberation and meaning and God are not to be discovered abstractly nor only within the narrow confines of the human spirit, but outwardly, bodily, involved with others in the same quest within social structures as well as in the quiet of one's heart and in the depth of the spirit. He had friends, talked with his disciples about his hopes, encouraged them to make their own decisions with regard to law, ignored social customs when they restricted relationships and also retreated to the mountains to pray, alone. The interior sense of freedom is conditioned by exterior freedom. Social freedom always includes the encounter with other free people, and with God.

HOW JESUS DIED

JESUS had a unique personal experience of God. The core of his message depends on the presence of the saving God in his personal history—this God who is mindful of the human race. Understanding Jesus, then, involves an appreciation of God's care for all people in human history. The disturbing point, however, in the life of Jesus as well as in all human lives, is the presence of signs that appear to contradict the loving care of God. How can we deal with the suffering and death of the Lord? The attitude of Jesus, his words and actions, how he faced suffering and the experience of his death have caused people to rethink the meaning of suffering.[14] The pain of Jesus, his crucifixion, did not

lter his awareness of the saving presence of God and
he nearness of his kingdom. This impels us to examine
ailure and pain.

In the midst of terrible human suffering, Jesus trusted
n the salvation and power and goodness of his Father.
The death of Jesus, however it might appear, was not a
ailure. Jesus died as he lived: he trusted in God and
elieved that eventually liberation, salvation and free-
lom would be accomplished.

An alternative to the Christian response to suffering
nd death considers life itself an illusion and concludes
hat people die as they live—in absurdity. The early
Christians, however, believed that in the case of Jesus
he benevolent God had the final word, since they also
rofessed that Jesus was raised from the dead. In his
lying the Lord committed himself in trust to God. He
id not renege on his teaching. Death was the summa-
ion of his life, the culmination of his conscious choices
or the sake of others. He died as he lived. The value
udgments made in his ministry were all completed in
hat final decision to trust his life to the hands of his
oving Father. The outcome was not yet known, but
vas accepted in faith. The Father responded by raising
esus from the dead. With this action the suffering and
leath did not lose their significance, but were seen as
he prelude to the establishment of Jesus in power:

This Jesus, God raised up. . . . God has made him
both Lord and Christ, this Jesus whom you crucified.
(Acts 2:32, 34b.)

Suffering in life always causes problems. When a per-
on accepts Jesus, including his pain and death, he
nows that human suffering involves God. Israel, in its
acred books, records the divine pathos in its history.
Now, in Jesus, God is present in human suffering
hrough the experience of his Son. The sorrow we bear
rings redemption, since through the faithful accep-
ance of this suffering we can experience aspects of life

that are possible only through pain. Love is purified
pain; truth becomes imperative; mortality, limitati
and dependence increase in magnitude, loom over tl
sickbed and stand beside mourners. In faith we can al
believe that God knows all pain and sorrow and suffe
ing, for he has experienced the same in Jesus, his So

Happily, the crucifixion culminates in the resurre
tion[15]—but this final dimension of the meaning
Jesus cannot be separated from the totality of his lif
Belief in the risen Lord sees the continuity between th
proclamation of God's presence in word and action an
the universal significance of Jesus for all people. A
risen Lord, Jesus is not only vindicated by God; as rise
Lord his relationship to God is brought to completion
In his dying in love and obedience to the Father, Jesu
revealed the mystery of his relationship to God; and i
the resurrection the Father manifested his relationshi
to Jesus. Jesus had committed himself to the Father i
his life and then in his death. When the Father raise
him, the Father manifested his eternal commitment i
return.

We also believe that the resurrection manifests libera
tion from earthly limitations; but the content of this lil
eration depends upon an appreciation of the earthly lif
of Jesus. The two cannot be separated. A risen Lor
separated from his earthly life is mythical; an earthl
Jesus separated from the risen Lord is another huma
failure. Only through the reciprocal relationship be
tween the two realities does it become clear that the re
urrection founds all our faith in the earthly Jesus as th
human face of God.

The followers of Jesus experienced the risen Lord. A
a result of these experiences they gathered together t
become the foundation of the Christian communit
which became the Church. Properly speaking, the resu
rection created faith in Jesus as the human face of Go
because only in terms of the risen Lord could one spea
of the exaltation of the earthly Jesus and appreciate th

ivine transcendence that was present all through his
fe.

We know that the gospels contain formulas or ex-
ressions of faith in which there is some appreciation of
he divinity of Jesus, but these must be seen as attempts
n the part of the early believers to remember in a cre-
tive way what Jesus said and did and then understand
he meaning involved. After the resurrection the disci-
les could see the relationship of many of the events of
he life of the Lord which they had personally wit-
essed. Now they could see him as the human mani-
station of the divine. His mission revealed the Father,
ut this was understood only in the light of the resur-
ection. Since God raised Jesus from the dead, his
arthly life took on an importance greater than what his
ollowers could have understood during their actual ex-
erience of his public ministry.

The early believers had to identify faith in the risen
ord with faith in the man Jesus: the raised and exalted
hrist of faith had to be seen in continuity with the
esus of history. We can say that the disciples with their
aster faith creatively recalled the major events in the
fe of Jesus and recognized them as manifestations of
he divine. The teachings, the way he treated others,
ere now related to the presence of the divine. The
postles saw the ordinary events in the life of Jesus
hrough an additional dimension: the human reflected
he divine. They looked upon Jesus and recognized the
resence of God.

This Easter faith, however, was not newly created by
he experience of the risen Lord without a support in
he historical experience of Jesus. The foundation in the
arthly experience of Jesus by his followers was per-
ected and understood only through the resurrection.
Ve can compare the faith of the disciples with ordinary
uman faith, which grows from the fundamental intu-
tion to the point of full acceptance. You meet some-
ne; you like him, feel comfortable in his presence; you

talk; you begin to confide in him; finally you believe i that person and trust him with your life. Such a thin occurred with Jesus and his disciples in his ministry, bu the resurrection led them to the fullness of faith in hi so that we can easily say that the Easter event was th principal basis for his followers' faith in Christ.

As with faith in Christ, so also the understanding c faith in Christ must be based upon the resurrectior Our theological appreciation of Jesus as the human fac of God will depend upon our acceptance of the resur rection. Christology is founded on the Easter even which involves not just what happened to Jesus, bu what happened to the followers of Jesus. The Easter ex perience lies in the assembling of the disciples in th name of Jesus and in the power of the risen Lord i their midst. The resurrection and the assembling ar two facets of one event: Jesus is present to his disciple in a new way—as one who has been accepted by th Father and thus has been changed in the relationship h has to his followers.

In the light of this experience, the disciples inter preted certain sayings of Jesus theologically, as well a those of the Old Testament. The meaning of the deat of Jesus was also understood in the light of the resur rection and the same could be said of the new appreci ation of the Old Testament notion of the messiah. Eve the cosmic theology of Philippians and Colossians i founded on the resurrection. Only after his resurrectior when he is Lord in power, does he reign over all (Co 1:15). The resurrection manifests the conviction of th Christian Church that, in Jesus as risen Lord, the divin presence has taken a human form in history. This hu man form, the earthly Jesus, has now been accepte by the Father as the final and eschatological manifes tation of the Father's concern for humankind.

The problem that plagues any study of Christology i the precise relationship between the human dimensior and the divine.[16] We cannot allow the loss of any o esus' humanness, nor can there be a loss of the divine. With difficulty we speak of two components, or two realities. Rather we should be conscious of two aspects of the one reality. When we speak of Jesus as the human face of God, it would not be correct to regard the human person of Jesus as taken up into the Logos. Such statements would convey the idea that Jesus was constituted as a human being and was then taken over by the person of the Logos. The problem lies in the inability to find language that can speak about two total aspects of one reality. We are trying to deal with the question of how Jesus, as a human person, also can be called the Son of God. Even the use of the "also" gives pause, since it, too, implies a separation rather than a unity in the reality.

We believe that in his humanity Jesus intimately lives with the Father and by virtue of this intimacy he is the Son. The center of his being as a man reposes not in himself, but in God the Father. The center, the support, even what we might call the heart of his personality consists in his relationship to God. Jesus was constitutively related and oriented to God as Father and was at the same time related to people as brother, as the bringer of salvation and the saving presence of God. Jesus possessed this unique combination and that is what makes him distinctive and gives him his identity. His autonomy as Jesus of Nazareth is his constitutive total relation to the one whom he calls Father: the God whose special concern is with the human race.[17]

When we ask from whence this experience arose, we are once again thrown back into the milieu of Judaism under Roman domination. Every human experience, even if thought original, stands in a tradition of social experience. No individual ever draws upon potential inner strengths alone. The consciousness of Jesus was like that of any other human being who lived within the Judaic tradition in Palestine. His experience of God was nurtured by his Jewish traditions as well as by his

human awareness of creatureliness and dependence. U
like his contemporaries, however, he was more co
cerned with proclaiming the saving nearness of G
than his eschatological judgment. It was this savi
presence that he identified with himself. Unless
suffered illusions, the only explanation was that G
had manifested in Jesus his saving presence in a fin
and definitive way. His followers in fact reacted in th
way. In Jesus the divine disclosed itself in a creature
and human way so that we might call this an instan
of human transcendence, or transcending humanity
even eschatological humanity. But even here we ca
never forget that no manifestation equals the realit
Jesus discloses the divine transcendence and also ve
God, since the created can never adequately reveal
unveil the infinite.

We can continue this discussion only by involving th
various efforts to give a firmer philosophical groun
work to the relationship and the presence of these tw
total aspects of the one reality of Jesus. The wor
of Rahner,[18] Schoonenberg,[19] Hulsbosch,[20] Schill
beeckx,[21] Küng[22] and others attempt to deal with th
question on a philosophical ground. The agreement th
they seem to have reached accepts as fundamental th
model of Jesus as the human face of God, or the sacr
ment of God, or the human manifestation of the divin
or God in Man. In each instance the theologian tries
break out of the more traditional approaches to Chri
tology as already seen in the model of Jesus as the Se
ond Person of the Blessed Trinity. They try to prese
other models based upon Scripture and human exper
ence as well as contemporary philosophy.

For our purposes, it is enough to appreciate that a
these theologians deal with the fundamental model
Jesus as the human face of God. In him, in his ov
person, is revealed both the eschatological (the fin
the ultimate, the irrevocable) face of all humanity a
the trinitarian fullness of God's being. Jesus being

man is God translated for us in a human fashion. His existence for others sacramentalizes among us the proexistence of God or the self-giving of God to his creatures. He is God for us and with us. His unique universality lies in Jesus' eschatological humanity, as the sacrament of God's love for all. In forgetfulness of self, Jesus identified himself with God's cause, which at the same time was the cause of all people. Thus Jesus lives as the firstborn of many brethren, since he is the one leaven for humanity which now participates in a different way in the life of the divine.

Jesus did not bring a new system, a new way of being human, a new way of living divorced from the ordinary experience of all people. Every individual has a wealth of possibilities, since in every person there is the potential for manifesting the presence of the divine. Jesus reminded us of this. Nothing that is human is foreign to God. Because of this human richness, the salvation offered by Jesus can never be translated completely into an all-inclusive system. The human face of God revealed in Jesus allows the possibility of many other expressions in other human faces. Everyone has the spark of the divine that the coming of Jesus has recalled. Everyone, without exception, is created in the image and likeness of God. Jesus revealed the presence of God in himself, but also reminded all people of their potential to reveal the divine. In him people can see God and also can see their own possibilities.

> —for Christ plays in ten thousand places,
> Lovely in limbs, and lovely in eyes not his
> To the father through the features of men's faces.[23]

ADVANTAGES

THE ADVANTAGES of such a model are evident at every turn. It emphasizes the totality of Jesus of Naz-

areth as the expression and revelation of God. There i
no aspect of his life forgotten or unimportant, so we
cannot concentrate on the cross or resurrection or any
other single moment without relating that event to the
other episodes of his life. Certain moments were, of
course, more significant than others, but we must al
ways look for the full revelation of God.

Secondly, such a model relates Jesus to the ordinary
experience of human life. Because we believe that Jesus
expressed the divine in the ordinary events of human
life, we can even identify with Jesus as the messiah and
Lord in power. People need not feel divorced from the
sacred as long as they can believe that this historical
person, in every aspect of his life, showed us the divine
People can study any dimension of his life through con
templating the New Testament and find some meaning
for themselves as they try in turn to manifest the divine
in their personal history. By reading prayerfully the
pages of his history, his followers discover what lie
hidden behind the words.

Thirdly, no false dichotomy exists between the hu
man and the divine. We do not take two elements and
try to make a third; rather, one reality expresses the
other. This profoundly influences all levels of theology
If the human can express the divine, then human life
has a value that can never be eliminated or forgotten in
spite of all attempts to denigrate it. The human face of
God affects Christian anthropology as well as question
related to morality and the meaning of the Church
Ecclesiology in particular is affected, since there is a
parallel in the understanding of Jesus as the human face
of God and the Church as the sacrament of Jesus in the
world today. This involves every aspect of the Church
not just its hierarchy and sacraments. Where the
Church is, Jesus is. The praying Church, the consoling
Church, the reconciler, the lover of truth, the patron of
the arts, the teaching Church, the serving Church
fulfills its destiny as the presence of Jesus in the world

today. The very human Church reflects the divine Jesus.

This model also restores a sense of balance in Christianity, which in the past often emphasized the spiritual to the detriment of the material. Since it was believed that the meaning of Jesus centered on his divinity, an individual was thought to be more like Jesus the more he or she concentrated on the spiritual. If the human is the expression of the divine, however, then the material aspect of human life is equally important as the spiritual. Both are vehicles that reveal the divine. The bodily aspect of humanity cannot be disparaged, since it mediates the divine and offers the divine an expression in space and time.

The model of Jesus as the human face of God also prevents the concentration on the future fulfillment of Christianity that would lead us to forget the present reality. If Jesus is the human face of God in history and if human history bears his stamp, then what is taking place now has great consequences for the human race. Salvation is not something reserved for the end of time. We experience the saving presence of God now in a human form. The fullness to come will ratify and perfect what is already present.

When one reads the New Testament it is clear that the model of Jesus as the human face of God is in full accord with Scripture. In the gospel of John, Jesus tells his disciples that he who sees him sees the Father (Jn. 14:9). Throughout the ministry of Jesus, people recognized that the power of God was present in his life. He revealed the concern of God for people in all of the episodes that are recorded in the gospels. They could look upon him and come to an appreciation of God. The gospels show the divine element of Jesus, but never apart from its human manifestation. Even the gospel of John, which stresses the divinity of Jesus more than any other of the New Testament writings, always joins divinity to the human dimension. The Logos becomes *flesh;* God's Son is the Son of Joseph; the powerful " am" is also bread, wine, shepherd.

Finally, such a model has important pastoral implica tions. If theologians speak of Jesus as the human fac of God, they can avoid a great deal of philosophica terminology, which most people do not understand an have no interest in trying to understand. At the sam time, the model offers much grist for the mills of thos who want to analyze it philosophically, especially i light of the development of personalism and other hu man approaches to philosophy.

Accepting Jesus as the human face of God also help believers to relate to and identify with the Lord withou having to worry about theories. Christology, then, is nc divorced from ordinary life and relegated to the lectur halls of academia. People can relate to it, since it in cludes in its purview the whole of human experience; a the human face of God, Jesus makes present the divin without ever abandoning our own finite existence. Fo the person concerned with the spiritual life, the life c faith, an appreciation of this model offers vast possi bilities for maturing as a Christian. This represent "practical" theology at its best and is sufficient reaso alone to pursue and develop this model.

LIMITATIONS

OF COURSE, the model also has weaknesses. The grea danger is that with the emphasis on the human as th expression of the divine, the signified can be lost in th sign. If the human expresses the divine, and if we there fore concentrate on the manifestation as very much par of ordinary human experience, then why continue t talk about the divine at all? Why not just see Jesus as good person who leads people to understand somethin about their personal lives? Or, granted that Jesus is con sidered to be the presence of the divine, how indis pensable is the divine, since all we can know about it i

ts human aspect? Might it not be true that the value of
Jesus rests on how he lived his human life, apart from
any relationship to the divine?

All of these deviations are possible. When the human
is overemphasized the divine will fall into the shadows
and concern for the divine can even disappear. Some
people, Gandhi for example, can bypass the divine completely and still make a plausible case in favor of the
value of Jesus and Christianity. They often use as their
starting point the value of Jesus as exemplifying the
best of humanity. Such people fail to see the intimate
link between the human and the divine as fundamental
to all life, and specifically to the life of Jesus.

Another problem is the possible loss of the afterlife.
Christianity has always presented a doctrine of a future
life, not only as a vindication of a life on earth well-
lived, but as the reward for such a life. To be with God
in a complete and total way captures that goal. Now, if
we see Jesus as the human face of God and emphasize
the divine reality that is already present in every person's life, the sense of a future life may also fall into
the background and disappear.

Such a position avoids the pitfalls of sterile philosophical quests, but it can also, by the same token, become anti-intellectual. Lacking some clearly thought-out
philosophical foundation, any theological proposition
tends to become fluid and eventually loses credibility.
Most believers may choose to take a stance that avoids
philosophy, but this is not possible for the professional
theologian, who must seek out responses to fundamental questions. A theology not built on a sound
philosophical foundation will soon collapse. Certainly
efforts have been made to give a firm foundation to this
model of Jesus as the human face of God (see
Schoonenberg, Rahner, Schillebeeckx, etc.) but in no
case have they answered all the questions. The present
model lacks the clear philosophical response that theologians in the past have given on great Christological

topics. Disagreement runs too strong. The root questio
is, of course: Does this position maintain the sense o
divinity of Jesus as expressed in the official councils o
the Church?

Finally, the danger of pantheism looms large in th
background of this model. If Jesus is the human face o
God, and if every human person can display the divin
then God is present in every person—there *is* an *er
hypostasis* that is part of the human experience. If th
is true, what prevents Christians from being pantheists
Can people be identified with God? Yes, with qualifica
tions—but if we do away with the various distinctior
in God and concentrate on a human being as manifes
ing God, then why not finally settle for the presence o
God in the universe, or at least speak of God as th
collectivity of that which is present in a limited fashio
in individuals?

In spite of its limitations, there is no doubt that thi
model is the most fruitful of those we have proposed. I
merits being called not a model but a paradigm. It ar
swers more questions and lends itself to more conclu
sions than any other model we have discussed. Th
strengths are too strong and too well documented to b
ignored; the dangers, conversely, are probably so ur
likely to be realized that they need not cause alarm. I
for no other reason, since this theological position con
tributes so much to the spiritual life of the believe
often unconcerned with deep theological issues,
should be accepted as a paradigm that speaks to th
needs of both the speculative and practical theology o
today. When we see Jesus as the human face of God
our Christian life is enriched and faith takes on a ne
glow. The model excites and adds a new element to th
Christian pursuit of the meaning of Jesus.

NOTES

1. See K. Rahner, "Christianity Within an Evolutionary View of the World," *Theological Investigations*, vol. 5 (Baltimore: Helicon, 1965), pp. 173 ff; also *Theological Foundations*, pp. 208 ff.

2. See the comments by R. North concerning A. Hulsbosch in "Recent Christology and Theological Method," *Continuum*, vol. 7 (1969), pp. 63–77. See also Mark Schoof, "Dutch Catholic Theology: A New Approach to Christology," *Cross Currents*, vol. 22 (1973), pp. 415–27.

3. Karl Barth, *The Humanity of God;* also H. Küng, *On Being a Christian* (New York: Doubleday, 1976).

4. See P. Schoonenberg, *The Christ* (New York: Herder and Herder, 1971); "God's Presence in Jesus: An Exchange of Viewpoints," *Theology Digest*, vol. 19 (1971), pp. 29–38; "Is Jesus 'Man plus God'?" *Theology Digest*, vol. 23 (1975), pp. 59–70, plus a letter from Schoonenberg, pp. 224–25. See also S. Pujdak, "Schoonenberg's Christology in Context," *Louvain Studies*, vol. 6 (1976), pp. 338–53.

5. J.A.T. Robinson, *The Human Face of God* (Philadelphia: Westminster, 1973).

6. See J. O'Grady, *Christian Anthropology* (New York: Paulist, 1976), Chapter 1.

7. E. Schillebeeckx, *Jesus: An Experiment in Christology* (New York: Seabury, 1979), p. 601.

8. It is true that in the gospel of Matthew Jesus speaks of "Our" Father (Mt. 6:9). This, however, is recognized by Scripture scholars as a liturgical formula, with the parallel place in Luke considered to be the original (Lk. 11:2).

9. See Mt. 11:27; Lk. 10:22; Mk. 13:32; Jn. 8:42, 10:25 ff, 12:49, 13:5, 10, 23, etc.

10. See William James, *The Variety of Religious Experience* (New York: Longman, Green, 1929) and R. Otto, *The Idea of the Holy* (New York: Oxford University Press, 1958).

11. The Christian understanding of original sin gives the theological foundation for this aspect of human life. See O'Grady, *Christian Anthropology*, Chapter 4, for a summary of the contemporary approaches to original sin.

12. Schillebeeckx, *Jesus: An Experiment in Christology*, p. 603.

13. See O'Grady, *Jesus, Lord and Christ,* pp. 10–16.

14. See Schillebeeckx, pp. 644–50; Rahner, *Theologica Foundations,* pp. 264–84; Rahner, *Theology of Death.*

15. Only recently in Roman Catholic theology has th Resurrection been seen in its pivotal position. Previously was viewed chiefly as the greatest of miracles and thus use in an apologetic sense. The renewal in resurrection theolog can be traced to the influence of the following: F. X. Du well, *The Resurrection* (New York: Sheed and Ward, 1960 and David Stanley, *Christ's Resurrection in Pauline S teriology* (Rome: Biblical Institute Press, 1961).

16. See the various critiques of some contemporary a proaches: A. Dulles, "Contemporary Approaches to Chri tology: Analysis and Reflections," *Living Light,* vol. 1 (1976), pp. 119–45; Thomas Clarke, "Current Christol gies," *Worship,* vol. 53 (1979), pp. 438–49; Gerald O'Co lins, "Jesus in Current Theology," *The Way,* vol. 16 (1976 pp. 291–308; Donald Gray, "The Divine and the Human i Jesus Christ," *CTSAP,* vol. 31 (1976), pp. 21–39; Pete Chirico, "Hans Küng's Christology: An Evaluation of I Presuppositions," *Theological Studies,* vol. 40 (1979), p 256–72.

17. It is this point that Schillebeeckx makes so well; se *Jesus: An Experiment in Christology,* pp. 657–61.

18. In addition to the works already cited, see "Curren Problems in Christology," *Theological Investigations,* vol. (Baltimore: Helicon, 1961), pp. 149–200 and "The Theol ogy of the Incarnation," *Theological Investigations,* vol. (Baltimore: Helicon, 1966).

19. The chief weakness of Schoonenberg is his apparen lack of a philosophical foundation. See the works cite above for a critique and his reaction.

20. Hulsbosch's work is known mainly through secondar sources. In addition to the works cited above, see R. North "Soul-Body Unity and God-Man Unity," *Theological Stud ies,* vol. 30 (1969), pp. 63–77.

21. Schillebeeckx promises to complete his work on Chris tology with an additional volume. Presumably, the philo sophical foundations will be clarified in this work.

22. See the critiques of Küng as mentioned above.

23. Gerard Manley Hopkins, "As Kingfishers Catch Fire, in *A Hopkins Reader* (New York: Doubleday, 1966), p. 67

6

THE MAN FOR OTHERS

HE PUBLICATION OF *Honest to God*[1] in 1963 by
A.T. Robinson, Anglican Bishop of Woolwich, caused
reaction throughout the entire world. In this provoca-
ve book Robinson did for systematic Christology what
e has more recently accomplished in the study of the
ew Testament in *Can We Trust the New Testament?*[2]
oth books generated so much discussion on every side
aat they cannot be disregarded. The former produced
s own progeny in numerous articles which eventually
d to a book called *The Honest to God Debate*. Robin-
on freely admits his dependence on two twentieth-cen-
ary theologians, Paul Tillich and Dietrich Bonhoeffer.
illich's *Systematic Theology* was published in English
1953,[3] the same year that witnessed the publication
English of the *Letters and Papers from Prison* of
onhoeffer.[4] We can then view the publication of *Hon-
st to God* as a climax of much of the theological
ebate waged in Protestant circles for the previous
ecade.

No doubt the provocative Bishop of Woolwich had
uch to say to contemporary Christianity that needed
be said. Now, almost twenty years later, the book has
erhaps been pushed to the sidelines, but there are still
aany elements of the bishop's thought that have found
eir way into the mainstream of Christian thought. The

book fertilized the thinking of the Church far mo
than was expected.

Robinson entitled his fourth chapter "The Man f
Others." He created this expression by abridging
phrase in Bonhoeffer's *Letters and Papers from Priso*
"man existing for others, hence the crucified."[5] Sin
that time the phrase has been used frequently in Chr
tian discourse, even by Popes Paul VI and John Paul

As we continue the study of models of Jesus, it is e
sential that we deal with this concept and study t
writings of Robinson, but even more so those of I
source, Bonhoeffer, since both authors turned to th
model as an antidote to a prevalent Christology th
overemphasized the divinity of Jesus.

Robinson perceived an urgent need to rethink t
relationship between humanity and divinity precise
because it had tended to be onesided:

> To use an analogy, if one has to present the doctri
> of the person of Christ as a union of oil and wate
> then the early Church made the best possible attem
> to do so . . . But it is not surprising that in popul
> Christianity the oil and water separated and that o
> or other came to the top.[6]

Traditionally, as Robinson pointed out, an overer
phasis on the humanity tended to lead to positions th
the Church labeled as heretical or at least offensive; a
overemphasis on the divinity led to positions whic
were comfortably accommodated within orthodoxy, b
nevertheless shortchanged the humanity of Jesus. T
counteract such a tendency, Robinson chose to follo
some suggestions of Bonhoeffer[7] and spoke of Jesus
"The Man for Others."

Bonhoeffer was the chief architect of this model, an
to understand it as more than a clever slogan deman
an appreciation of Bonhoeffer's thought. Bonhoeff
sees the origin and continuing presence of evil in th
world as the breaking of the link between God and ou

elves, which led to the tearing of the very fabric of humanity. The human race has been wounded interiorly by the presence of evil. People live and die painfully experiencing the sense of incompletion and the rending of what was meant to be whole. The savior would restore the torn fabric of humanity through the reconciliation of everyone with God. For Bonhoeffer, the Church is the *locus* where the fabric is restored and where people experience the reconciling presence of Christ.

For Bonhoeffer, the meaning of Jesus was not to be found so much in the study of his being, or through an ontological analysis of his relationship to God; rather he must be seen and understood in a functional way as the one by whom reconciliation is accomplished. He is savior, then, primarily as the man for others.

Applied to the Church, this model identifies the Christian community as a group within which the man for others continues his work of reconciling and restoring. The corollary of the view of Jesus as the man for others accomplishing the reconciliation and restoration is a Church continuing this mission through the activity of its members.

Bonhoeffer saw the community element of the Church as essential, since the result of the activity of Jesus as the man for others was the building of the sense of community. Christians now belong to each other in Christ; the individual believers need each other. The one who believes in Jesus relates to others just as the individual himself discovered Jesus through others. The Church is more than a place where the word is proclaimed and the sacraments are administered; it is also the place where the members of the community live in forgiveness and communion with each other precisely because of their understanding of Jesus as reconciler. Unless those who have been personally healed continue the mission of Jesus and see him as the one who offered himself to others, Christianity has no

meaning. This model intimately relates the mission
Jesus to the mission of the Church.

Many people associate Bonhoeffer with the notion
"religionless Christianity" and the end of the Churc
These ideas come from a letter he wrote to a frie
while he was in prison. The letter is largely made up
questions. No doubt his thought was in turmoil as
wrote, but he did not abandon his earlier view on
Church. He could not do that without abandoning
viewpoint on Jesus himself. Rather, in his perso
conflict he asks questions that are legitimate for
Church of every generation. He was led on by an
stinctive feeling for the questions that are bound
emerge rather than by any conclusions already reach

Robinson refers to the thought of Bonhoeffer as
"tantalizing intimation."[9] Bonhoeffer had planned
write a book on the questions he proposed, but his e:
cution by the Nazis prevented it. What he envision
was a Church different from the one he had expe
enced. He wanted a Church that would be the expr
sion of Christ in the world; an incarnation that en
sioned Christ not as the all-knowing divine Seco
Person of the Blessed Trinity, but as the man who ga
himself in his total existence for others. Practical the
ogy always had more of an interest for Bonhoeffer th
dogmatic theology. The formation and developm
necessary for the Christian—conformity to Jesus, w
was made man, crucified and raised from the dea
forms the foundation for his thought. The key verse
Bonhoeffer was Romans 12:2:

> Do not be conformed to this world but be tra
> formed by the renewal of your mind that you n
> prove what is the will of God, what is good and
> ceptable and perfect.

He further describes his Christology:

> Conformed with the incarnate—to be really man

*onformed with the crucified—to be man sentenced by
God
*onformed with the risen Lord—to be man before
God.[10]

*od first makes us human beings. Believers do not slav-
*hly imitate Christ so that they become spiritualized;
*eople first become human because God became human
*1 Jesus. Christ recreated the human form before God,
*nd he accomplished this in his attitude toward others.

The Church that flows from this model bears the
*orm proper to humanity. The community shows a
*uman image. The Church concerns itself with the
*hole person and with all of the implications of human
*fe. *Religion as the external expression of faith matters
ittle, but Christ shaping a community of people matters
*much. When people are conformed to the incarnate
*ne, they become what they really were meant to be.
*he really free person allows himself or herself to live
*s the creator's creature. When people refuse the con-
*ormity to Jesus they fail in their very being. Such
*houghts recall the remark of Camus that "Man is the
*nly creature who refuses to be what he really is."

Conformity to the Crucified One emphasizes that
*very person must be declared just by God and can do
*his only by dying the daily death of the sinner. The
*hristian learns to die to his or her personal will and
*ccept the suffering entailed. This experience of suffer-
*ng, which is intrinsically bound up with the service of
*thers, enables one to die to one's personal will by
*gladly committing oneself into a stronger hand.

Finally, the conformity to the risen Christ declares
*that every believer must be a new person before God.
*Bonhoeffer understood this in strongly biblical terms. In
*the midst of death the believer lives; in the midst of sin,
*he is righteous; in the midst of the old, he is new. The
*world notices none of this, for the new person lives in
*the world like any other person, apparently undistin-

guished from anyone else. The difference lies in the internal conformity to Jesus, which makes his follower more human and more closely bound to each other.

Like Luther, Bonhoeffer teaches the ethics of the cross rather than that of glory. People do not become God; rather God became human and thus we can become human in the Church, provided that we see Jesus as the man who existed for others and that we in turn fulfill a similar mission. In common with the reform tradition, Bonhoeffer finds Jesus in word and sacrament but especially in the community.[11] Bonhoeffer accepts a functional, rather than an ontological Christology. He concerns himself with who Jesus is in relationship to others, rather than with trying to explain just who Jesus is in himself. The German theologian could live with many unanswered questions, unlike those who have taken more traditional approaches to Christology, precisely because he studied Jesus in his relationship. When asked where Christ is, he responded:

> He is at the border of my experience,
>   where he gives meaning to my existence.
> He is at the center and is the meaning of history,
>   giving to history purpose and hope.
> He is at the heart of nature,
>   giving to all creation meaning and hope.[12]

Everyone who believes in Jesus discovers the presence of Christ in personal existence, in the movement of history and in the meaning of creation. All three become meaningful in Jesus because his existence was for others.

The mature thought of Bonhoeffer remains unclear. He never had the opportunity to develop his thinking beyond a rudimentary stage and his experience in a Nazi prison limited his perspective even more. Very often, however, the seeds of mature thoughts can be found in the earliest writings of a person; we can turn to some of Bonhoeffer's earlier concepts to get a clearer

erspective on his Christology. Such a procedure often
ccurs in the history of theology. The secretary of
homas Aquinas finished the *Summa Theologica* based
n earlier writings. As with those of Aquinas, these
oughts of Bonhoeffer remain incomplete, but they
ve a clear enough indication of the general direc-
on.[13]

In 1933 Bonhoeffer delivered a series of lectures on
hristology which he claims to have had more trouble
reparing than any other lectures he had delivered.
hese presentations marked the end of his regular aca-
emic work, since with the rise of Nazi Germany in the
icceeding years he would be more and more involved
ith the survival of the Confessing Church.

The fundamental theme of the Christology in these
ectures was the presence of Christ. With Harnack and
thers, he found it impossible to make the traditional
otion of the two natures the basis of his approach. For
onhoeffer, such a stance did not deal sufficiently with
he attempt to relate the meaning of Jesus to the con-
emporary scene. A retreat to past responses would
ever satisfy this theologian's need to break new
round. Also, his reform tradition reached beyond the
nore traditional approach to Christology and allowed
im to develop some modifications in what has come to
e called functional Christology.

Bonhoeffer chose not to use the historical Jesus as the
asis for his approach. The recent studies on the rela-
ionship between the Jesus of history and the Christ of
aith had caused so much confusion that only with
lifficulty could he base his approach on the actual his-
orical figure. Instead, he chose the only possible point
f departure that would fit his purpose. He returned to
he "for me" of the reform tradition.[14] Christ-for-me
loes not involve dogma nor literary-historical research
nto the gospels, but focuses on the Church as the expe-
ience of Jesus in relationship to others. The Christ
emembered, systematized and historicized actually be-

comes present and continues as the one whose existen is determined by his relationship to others. The lectur were divided accordingly: present Christ, historic Christ and future Christ. Unfortunately, the final secti remained unfinished.

The analysis of traditional Christology can cause t theologian and the believer to get bogged down in met physical speculation. To know Christ, said the r formers, is to know his blessing. Bonhoeffer believ firmly in this adage. He was aware of the eternal my tery that surrounds the historical manifestation of Go but believed that the understanding of this mystery not found through philosophy, but rather by the th ologian asking the questions "What?" and "Where' rather than the question "How?" What is Jesus for m Where can I find him? These questions carry great significance than the how of Jesus' person. The respon to these two previous questions clarifies the mystery be ter than the question of how, since no one can ev come to grips with the question of how in an adequa sense. Even with the limitations placed upon the r sponse to these questions, the possible answers can le; to a deeper personal understanding of Jesus and h relationship to the individual, which is more importa than any effort to try to settle the question of how tl mystery is possible.

Bonhoeffer believed that Jesus discloses himself Word and sacrament and that he also lives in tl Church. As the Word, he is God's address to peop and hence demands a response.[15] No communicatio exists unless the receiver listens and responds. Tl Word of God addressed to humankind implies a rel tionship that will bind Jesus as the expression of tl thought of God to those who have learned of God fro Jesus in his Church and have responded. We can ta about Jesus as the revelation of God, but that revelatio remains incomplete until people accept it.

Bonhoeffer also sees this Word present in the co

uing life of the Church. The community proclaims
e Word of God and expects a response from the lis-
ners. Believers in Jesus speak the Word of God now,
en though the ultimate human expression of the
ord of God was in Jesus. Followers of Jesus must
entify this human word as the Word of God and can
o so only in the context of the Church. There exists
e right question and one right answer. The question is
und in the proclamation of the Church and the an-
ver is found in the personal and individual response of
e person who hears.

Christ is also sacrament.[16] Bonhoeffer demands that
I ask the question "Who is present in the sacrament?"
he response: Jesus Christ, the God-Man, in his exalta-
on and his humiliation is present in the sacrament.
esus is really present, not just represented in the sacra-
ent; only one who is absent needs to be represented.
onhoeffer's thought joins Jesus' presence in the sacra-
ent to his presence in the Church. As the Word he
eaks to create the Church and as sacrament Christ as-
mes a bodily presence in a ritual meal, but only be-
use the Church already exists as his body. Just as the
Vord demands a response to complete the relationship,
o too with the Eucharist. The celebration of sacrament
resupposes the presence of the Church and of Jesus as
e one given for others. Only in this way can he be
resent in a ritual meal, again defining his mode of
eing as of one whose existence is for the sake of
thers. Who is Jesus of Nazareth must of necessity
oint also to the question "What is Jesus? Jesus is the
Vord that is offered to others; Jesus is the sacrament
aat is offered to others; Jesus is the Church that exists
s the result of the acceptance of what is offered."[17] We
an develop this thought further not by asking the ques-
on "How?" but by asking "Where?" I have already
nentioned Bonhoeffer's response to this question. Fur-
ner analysis will help us understand just how well
.obinson's use of the title "The Man for Others" sums

up the particular theological perspective that both Bo
hoeffer and Robinson consider to be necessary for
model of Jesus.

Jesus stands on the border of my existence, beyo
my existence and for me.[18] Jesus offers to people t
possible discovery of their authentic existence a
forms the boundary of that existence. As the mediat
Jesus restores the torn fabric of humanity and acco
plishes a reconciliation between God and us. When i
dividuals turn and seek a sense of peace and unity wi
God they experience reconciliation. Authentic hum
existence can be discovered only when forces with
and without an individual allow for a healing of the i
ternal spirit as well as of external relationships. Jesus
the one who offers himself for others in his minist
and fulfills his mission of mediator in his death and re
urrection offers us the possibility of accomplishing
our own lives and in our own human experience a sin
lar sense of well-being and healing. He has alrea
fulfilled the one true law of human existence in rel
tionship to others, which people had been unable a
unwilling to fulfill. Jesus stands eternally as judgme
on the human failure to meet the demands of the law
human existence through an acceptance of the law
love. He stands at the border of my existence, calli
me to seek and find fulfillment; he stands beyond m
since I still struggle with the forces that are alien
human life; and he stands before me to help me achie
the human possibilities that are present in every life. I
lives for me and for my existence.

HE IS THE CENTER OF HISTORY

HISTORY expresses the universal expectation of a me
siah, someone who would come to heal all of the br
ken dreams, and fulfill all of the shattered promise
who would bring a sense of hope and a longing for
future which is more than just a repetition of the u

appy past.[19] Jesus fulfills and at the same time destroys
all human expectations and hopes. He destroys them,
since the visible and triumphant messiah who would accomplish all of these hopes and expectations failed to
come; he fulfills them even though the sense of perfection and completion lies hidden in the human possibility
to learn from Jesus and accomplish in individual and
communal lives the power of healing and reconciliation
that creates the only true meaning of human life. This
has already happened, since Jesus has already given
himself to others. God has truly entered human history
and the expected one remains here, calling people to accept their personal responsibility to live the life based
upon a common and interdependent human existence.

This Christ, the center of human history, offers himself in Word and in sacrament and in the Church. The
Church thus becomes the center of history, since in this
community we have the actual experience of people
who are following the example of Jesus, who gave himself for others.

HE IS THE CENTER OF NATURE

IN THE original plan of God, nature was created to be
the Word of God, but it has been enslaved through the
guilt of human beings.[20] Nature does not need reconciliation, but is in need of liberation. Christ in his
Church announces the liberation of nature as seen in
the sacraments, for elements of the old and fallen creation have now become part of the new creation. The
Church in its sacramental practice speaks for muted nature and proclaims the creative Word to believers.

Human existence, human history and nature are
closely connected in the thought of Bonhoeffer. Human
life is always history and always nature. As the fulfiller
of the law, of human hopes and expectations, of the
demands of love, and as liberator of creation, the mediator performed these tasks for all of human existence.

Jesus lived first as the mediator for me, for all people but in so being he accomplished the purpose of human history through reconciliation and healing; he is the end of the old world and the beginning of the new world in God. Jesus frees nature from the bonds of human sin and guilt, and nature then becomes the additional means to proclaim the Word of God. Existence on behalf of the human race also includes a personal offering to human history and the liberation of all of creation.

Bonhoeffer criticized the obsession of the "how" Christology of traditional definitions, but he admitted the need for dogma in Christianity. He set out to study the various heresies in Christian history and concluded that a once-for-all, univocal declaration about Jesus Christ is illegitimate: theologians should not speak of the divinity and humanity as objects. The question "how" raises too many problems with which it cannot cope, but it will lead inevitably to the more pressing questions of "Who is Jesus for me?" and "What does he do for me?"

Still, Bonhoeffer appreciated the need for dogma. Through his reflection on the New Testament, he found two most evident and most demanding themes which can form the basis for the Christian dogma of Christ: the incarnate one and the humiliated and exalted one.

THE INCARNATE ONE

THEOLOGIANS may describe Jesus as God, but they must go beyond the divine essence in which Jesus participates when they attempt to explain this concept. We cannot try to study his omnipotence or his all-encompassing knowledge or his eternity, but rather must speak of the man among sinners; the incarnate one whose life included the manger and the cross.[21] The study of Christology involves the entire historical Jesus and in this perspective theology declares that Jesus lived as the presence of God among people. In him the

reated recognizes the creator among themselves. The
nderstanding of Jesus as the presence of God depends
pon his human environment and relationships. As a
uman creature Jesus attained his glory, but under the
eil of the cross. To take seriously the incarnate one
emands an insertion of Jesus into the earthliness of
uman history. In that experience God manifested him-
elf and creation glorified him. Incarnation rests upon
n existence for others.

THE HUMILIATED AND EXALTED ONE

F THE incarnation involves a sense of humiliation, then
xaltation can be interpreted as a return of Christ from
he human sphere to the eternal life of God.[22] But in
his dichotomy, theologians often lose an appreciation
f the meaning of Christ. The humiliation and the exal-
ation cannot be separated into two moments; they both
ust be predicated of the same incarnate one. Jesus is
ot exalted only in his resurrection. As the crucifixion
rings to a culmination the life that is offered to others
nd for the sake of others, so the resurrection completes
n experience of exaltation in humiliation. When Jesus
orgives his betrayer, prays for his persecutors, and
verlooks the abandonment by his apostles, God exalts
im in his lowliness. Following the example of Jesus,
nyone who loses his life actually saves it, not only in
he future but in the present.

The Church also lives by the power of his humilia-
ion and his exaltation. Daily it reenacts God's gift in
Christ, receiving the forgiveness of sins through the real
resence of the incarnate, humiliated and exalted one.
n him God enables the Church by faith to see the
eaning and purpose of life. The one who gave of him-
elf on behalf of others and in so doing brought about
he glorification of God and his own personal exaltation
ontinues to fulfill the same function in the Church.
esus is the man for others, found in Word, sacrament

and Church, who calls individuals as members of the holy community to continue his mission of being the incarnation of the self-offering God in human history. Jesus promises that in following his example men and women will discover the meaning of human existence when they care for each other, feed each other, clothe each other, share a common life that rejoices with the happy and sorrows with the burdened. Then they will experience the sense of exaltation in the actual living of the life of humiliation as they await the final exaltation on that last day, when the sense of the interrelated and interdependent will be manifested finally and irrevocably. Then God will be all in all. The man for others is indeed a model that speaks eloquently to the torn fabric of humanity and offers a possibility of restoration and healing.

ADVANTAGES

CHRISTOLOGY gains much in this model. In the history of Christianity people sometimes have lost sight of the actual meaning of the gospel and how it affects their personal lives. Jesus, viewed as the man for others who calls his followers to imitate him and to be for others themselves, makes clear the essential purpose of Christianity. A functional approach to Jesus allows the individual believer to live in such a way that the teaching of Jesus actually affects and is seen to affect the human condition. Francis of Assisi, Vincent de Paul and Mother Theresa of Calcutta are but a few of those whose faith has made them live for others.

Such a model also emphasizes the present reality as reward for a life well-lived, instead of emphasizing the eternal life to come. If people live their earthly existence oriented toward a relationship with others, then the present is stressed and future reward flows from it as the natural consequence of what has already taken place. Incarnation implies that God has taken an inter est in human history and is present not only in the future but today. Jesus the incarnate one has dignified the human enterprise with his presence, so the daily task of living carries with it a spiritual value that should be appreciated and enjoyed.

The appreciation of Jesus as the man for others also gives to Christian ethics its proper perspective. The believer does not live life accumulating merit; he or she lives life in relationship to others who are trying to better the human condition. An ethics of the cross will be the price paid, but the cost will be more than compensated for by the result—the continual discovery of true human existence. The experience of Bonhoeffer during the period of Nazi Germany helped him to appreciate the need for a determined Christian ethic that would encompass not only the experience of practical living for others but the discovery of authentic existence as well.

This model also helps to disclose what it means to be human. People are forever searching for a personal meaning in life. They ask the question often: "What does life mean?" Jesus, as the man for others, assures those believers who follow him that they will arrive at the discovery of the true human existence. This involves more than a concern for the spiritual aspect of the person; true human life involves all dimensions of the human personality. Physical, psychological, emotional and spiritual aspects must be appreciated and allowed to develop. Such a model enhances the potential already present in the lives of people and expands the field of human activity within the Christian economy. The new life of a person finds its fulfillment after living for others, just as the resurrected Lord found his fulfillment after a life and death offered for the sake of others.

To see Jesus as the man for others gives proper place to the meaning of Jesus in Scripture. The gospels portray Jesus as the one who frequently explained the

meaning of his life in relationship to others. He co
cerned himself with the poor, the sick, the oppresse
He offered not only a healing of soul but a healing
mind and body. Jesus responded to every aspect of
person's life and in each instance took people as the
were and tried to offer himself in service. "For the Sc
of Man has come not to be served but to serve and
give his life as a ransom for the many [Mk. 10:45]

Jesus as the man for others serves well the interest
the social needs of human life so common today. Bo
within and without the Church a new awareness post
lates that the survival of the human race depends upc
individuals becoming actively interested in each othe
particularly in those who experience economic, social
cultural oppression. The haves must care for the hav
nots. The tendency in the past to live in isolation h
been shaken by our sudden awareness that the huma
race lives precariously on this planet and that on
through cooperation and concern for every individu
can the human race hope to survive. Jesus, the indivi
ual who cared for the oppressed in every way, gives
added impetus for Christians to become involved in th
critical needs of society. At the same time, this model
lived effectively by Christians shows those who do n
believe that the Christian Church concerns itself wit
social problems and has taken an active role in trying
alleviate oppression. If Jesus had been seen as a ma
for others, perhaps some of the atrocities that have bee
perpetrated during the present century would have bee
resisted, if not wholly prevented. Christianity cannot r
treat to the safety of the sanctuary, precisely becaus
Jesus himself would allow no concern for person
safety to interfere with his service of others. With suc
a model in mind the Christian Church must reach ou
side of itself and embrace those who cry out in nee
even if at times this may mean an experience of pai
and suffering for the Church itself.

LIMITATIONS

THE WEAKNESSES of the model are also clear. Bonoeffer, Robinson and their followers tend to overlook the history of theology and the contributions that have been made in the past by great Christian theologians. A functional approach has value, but cannot be separated completely from an ontological one. We must ask not only what does Jesus mean to me but also what does he do for me. Christians must search out who Jesus is and how he is the Son of God and the savior of humankind. Theology before the middle of the twentieth century contained insights which should not be denied or overlooked. The emphasis of a more functional Christology tends to overlook these insights.

While our model emphasizes the role of Jesus as servant, which is surely present in the New Testament, it does not deal sufficiently with other lines of thought in the New Testament. Jesus is also the Son of the Father; he made it clear that his relationship to God was different from the relationship that others had to God. The New Testament has not one Christology, but many. The approach of Mark, where Jesus is seen as the suffering Son of Man who does not seek personal vindication, remains as true as the approach of Luke, where Jesus appears as the perfect Greek gentleman, calm and compassionate, dedicated to God and filled with his spirit, testified to by his life of prayerful contemplation. The views of Matthew and John must also be included. They both set forth in various degrees the servant theme, but they also see Jesus as the exalted Lord of all, who demands reverence and homage. Thus our present model picks up one biblical theme but overlooks others. Even in the use of the New Testament for this model, those authors could have benefited from a closer study of the Scriptures to include other aspects of the servant theme, thus giving a fuller appreciation of its meaning.

To be servant means to be united with those whom c
serves. This sense of unity with those in need, as
scribed in the New Testament, could have been used
a firmer foundation for the model of Jesus as the m
for others.

After the widespread concern for the poor and
oppressed in the 1960s and early 1970s, theologi
judged this "welfare" effort to be much needed but
the same time onesided. Christianity must be involv
with the poor, but it has no ready answers for the soc
problems of the world. The poor we shall always ha
with us, and even in the midst of poverty the gospel c
and must be preached. Those who believe in Christ
not fundamentally social workers, but preachers of
good news. Seeing Jesus as the man for others can
courage certain believers to see the mission of
Church primarily or even exclusively in terms of soc
justice. The tension that will always exist between
mission of the gospel to proclaim the good news
God's saving presence in human history and the missi
to alleviate the plight of those who are suffering becau
of a lack of justice is healthy and ought not to be elir
nated. The Jesus who is found in the poor is also ce
brated in the Eucharist, and they are not two differe
entities. Only when the model of Jesus as the man
others is joined with other models can this creative te
sion be sustained.

A further problem with such a model is that it ten
to obscure the meaning and reduce the importance
the institutional Church. If any person who lives his
her life for the sake of others in imitation of Jesus liv
the full meaning of discipleship, then an organiz
Church has little purpose. Not without basis do sor
cite Bonhoeffer as a basis for rejecting organized re
gion. His own comments on "religionless Christianit
fit in here with his theology of Jesus as the man
others. But without some support from an organiz
body, the impetus to fulfill the mission of Jesus as t

one for others can often become dissipated and actually die. For survival in this cruel and often evil world, Christians need the sense of community that comes only in the commitment to an organized Church.

No doubt the model of Jesus as the man for others has much to say to the contemporary believer. It offers insights into the meaning of Jesus and helps translate his meaning into the practical elements of human life. After years of an overemphasis on the divinity of Jesus, the model of the man for others offers a corrective. At the same time it should not be seen as *the* paradigm. It answers some of the questions and responds to some of the problems, but it can by no means encompass the wealth of insights that have been part of the Christian tradition. Jesus still remains, however, the man for others, his life given for the many. The true believer must learn from this model and put into practice its implications. The strength of the model is also its weakness: it presents an often-forgotten dimension of Christology, but one that can obscure other aspects. The model of the man for others is helpful and most needed, even if it cannot serve as a paradigm.

NOTES

1. J.A.T. Robinson, *Honest to God* (Philadelphia: Westminster, 1963). See also E. Routley, *The Man for Others* (New York: Oxford University Press, 1964).

2. J.A.T. Robinson, *Can We Trust the New Testament?* (Grand Rapids, Mich.: Eerdmans, 1977). This work has not met with the same enthusiasm as the previous work.

3. P. Tillich, *Systematic Theology* (Chicago: University of Chicago Press, 1951–66).

4. D. Bonhoeffer, *Letters and Papers from Prison,* rev. ed. (New York: Macmillan, 1967).

5. *Ibid.,* pp. 209–10.

6. Robinson, *Honest to God,* p. 65.

7. See D. Bonhoeffer, *Christ the Center* (New York: Harper & Row, 1960); *The Cost of Discipleship* (New

York: Macmillan, 1967); *Creation and Fall* (New York: Macmillan, 1966); *Ethics* (New York: Macmillan, 1964); *The Communion of Saints* (New York: Harper & Row, 1963). See also John Phillips, *Christ for Us in the Theology of Dietrich Bonhoeffer* (New York: Harper & Row, 1967); and B. Reise, *The Promise of Bonhoeffer* (Philadelphia: Lippincott, 1969).

8. See Bonhoeffer, *Letters and Papers from Prison*, pp. 151–57.

9. Robinson, *Honest to God*, p. 75.

10. Bonhoeffer, *Christ the Center*.

11. *Ibid.*, pp. 49–60.

12. *Ibid.*, pp. 61–68.

13. See J. Pelikan, "The Early Answer to the Question Concerning Jesus Christ: Bonhoeffer's Christology of 1933" in M. Marty, *The Place of Bonhoeffer* (New York: Association Press, 1962), pp. 147–66.

14. Bonhoeffer, *Christ the Center*, p. 47.

15. *Ibid.*, pp. 49–53.

16. *Ibid.*, pp. 53–59.

17. *Ibid.*, pp. 59–61.

18. *Ibid.*, pp. 62–67.

19. *Ibid.*, pp. 63–66.

20. *Ibid.*, pp. 66–67.

21. *Ibid.*, pp. 106–10.

22. *Ibid.*, pp. 110–18.

7

JESUS, PERSONAL SAVIOR

THE EXPERIENCE OF ten thousand Christians gathered in
one place and singing together: "Jesus is Lord" can
create a moment that will live forever in memory. Pentecost 1975 offered such a moment. Believers from all
over the world—Roman Catholic and Protestant, people from main-line denominations as well as from evangelical groups—gathered in Rome at St. Peter's and expressed in an enthusiastic outburst their personal and
communal conviction that they had experienced the
presence of the Lord in their lives. Jesus was their personal savior. The Spirit had been given and they had
been baptized in the Spirit to declare the wonderful insights and blessings of the Christian faith to all.

Since the late Sixties this new enthusiastic movement
has swept across the United States and other countries and carried with it a host of devotees. Lives are
changed; decisions are made for Christ; commitments
are forged; personalities are altered; barriers are broken
down; hopes and expectations are fulfilled. Millions of
people have shared in the new outpouring of the Holy
Spirit and come to know Jesus as their savior. Whether
we describe these people as Pentecostals, Charismatics,
born-again Christians or Evangelicals, there can be no
doubt that a new phenomenon has hit the Church and
for the first time what we had previously associated
with an evangelical, fundamentalist type of Christianity

has found a place in Roman Catholic circles as well
in the main-line Protestant churches.

This movement has created a flourishing number
prayer groups all over the world. People gather week
or daily to express in communal prayer their convicti
that they have experienced the wonders of God. Sen
nars are conducted for the uninitiated on the meani
of Baptism in the Spirit, in reading of the Word of G
and on the ministry of healing. Daily the numbe
grow; the groups cross all denominations. Charles Co
son, once involved in Watergate, now born again in t
Spirit, appears on the same platform with former U
Senator Harold Hughes as well as Terence Cardin
Cooke, retired General Ralph Haines, Ruth Carte
Stapleton and Archbishop Helder Camara of Brazil.[1]

The conviction of the group that the Lord liv
among them leads them to see his presence in all
their decisions, both personal and communal:

> Through a long process of discernment which has i
> volved many leaders from the region, the Lord ma
> it clear that he is commissioning his people to con
> to New York City where his love will overflow in
> special word about the poor and social justice . .
> We believe the Lord wants to fill the stadium wi
> persevering and hungry for God brothers and sister
> By his grace that's who we are.[2]

For these Christians the model on which believe
should base their faith is that of Jesus as the person
savior of all, coming into lives through the gift of t
Spirit and making a radical change. The person makes
total commitment to the reality of the gospel of t
Lord. No one acquainted with this Christian phenom
non of the late twentieth century can deal with t
meaning of Jesus without some appreciation of t
charismatic movement and the image of Jesus it pr
sents.

THE MEANING OF ENTHUSIASM

IN 1949 Ronald Knox published the book *Enthusiasm*.[3] In the first chapter he writes of the choice of possible titles for his work and claims that he settled for *Enthusiasm*, "not meaning thereby to name (for name it has none) the elusive thing that is its subject. I have only used a cant term, pejorative and commonly misapplied as a label for a tendency."[4] Knox's purpose is to offer an understanding of a recurrent theme in the history of Christianity whereby certain individuals choose to live a less worldly life, or seek to restore the earlier experience of the Church, or allow the full presence of the Spirit of Jesus to guide their lives.

In the history of the Church very often these movements attempted a fresh approach to religion. What had been an external and often empty form of observance now became an affair of the heart involving the entire person.

Sacraments are not necessarily dispensed with but the emphasis lies in a direct personal access to the Author of our salvation with little intellectual background or liturgical expression . . . An inward experience of peace and joy is both the assurance which the soul craves for and its characteristic prayer attitude.[5]

The author treats some of the characteristics of the movement that have recurred in history: often there is ecstasy, prophecy, people breaking out into unintelligible utterance, identified at times by expert evidence as a language unknown to the speaker.[6]

Throughout the book Knox examines the enthusiastic movements that have recurred in the Christian tradition, but it must be admitted that his personal position toward them is not one of "enthusiasm." In the last paragraph of his final chapter, Knox affirms that the institutional perspective of the Roman Catholic Church does not mean that it lacks all spiritual initiative. The Church maintains the new as well as the old. Then he admits the danger in such an institutional position:

> Where wealth abounds it is easy to mistake shadow for substance; the fires of spirituality may burn low and we go on unconscious, dazzled by the glare of tinsel suns. How nearly we thought we could do without St. Francis, without St. Ignatius. Men will not live without vision; that moral we do well to carry away with us from contemplating in so many strange forms the record of the visionaries.[7]

His final line is a quotation from *La Princesse lointaine*:

> Frère Trophime: Inertia is the only vice,
>   Master Erasmus, and the only virtue.
> Erasmus: Why?
> Frère Trophime: Enthusiasm.[8]

Jesus as personal savior creates enthusiasm and has remained in this role throughout history as an integral part of Christianity. This model needs to be explored because for many the savior is most personal and thus most important.

BIBLICAL FOUNDATIONS

THE New Testament itself shows no great interest in the meaning of redemption, but the Old Testament background of this notion colors any sense of salvation and savior.[9] Redemption in the Old Testament refers principally to the "buying back" of the firstborn dedicated to God (Ex. 34:20; Num. 18:15). Later, it refers to the action of God in redeeming Israel from the slavery of Egypt (Dt. 7:8, 24:18). In the later writings of the Old Testament redemption is transferred to the individual whose redemption equals liberation (Jer. 15:10).[10]

The writers of the New Testament continue to use this Old Testament image, but with even greater emphasis on the aspect of liberation. The implications of buying back are almost never referred to, with the possible exception of Mark 10:45: "The Son of Man also came not to be served but to serve and to give his life as a ransom for many." Matthew takes this saying from Mark and incorporates it exactly into his account in 20:28. Perhaps the early Church had some notion of the buying back which then quickly fell into disuse. Even these passages, however, lack the notion of ransom that is often found in the medieval writers.[11]

We can conclude that while redemption was part of the background of the New Testament writers, they were not overly concerned with the notion as they tried to deal with Jesus as savior. The notion of liberation, however, is present because Jesus redeemed people from sin, from the "principalities and powers," from the law and death (Rom. 3:24; 1 Cor. 1:30; Eph. 1:7; Col. 1:14; Heb. 9:15). The one additional note from the New Testament congruent for our discussion on Jesus as savior is the conviction that Jesus died and rose for all. Jesus accomplished universal redemption (Phil. 3:10; Rom. 4:25; 1 Cor. 6:14; 2 Cor. 4:14).

The New Testament, however, frequently speaks of salvation and Jesus as savior. Jesus preaches salvation by the proclamation of the kingdom of God. With him God established a communion with his people which means that now they are saved. The gospel itself is the message of salvation: "To us has been sent the message of salvation [Acts 13:26]." It is the way of salvation: "These men are servants of the Most High God who proclaim to you the way of salvation [Acts 16:17]." It is the power of God for salvation: "For I am not ashamed of the gospel; it is the power of God for salvation to everyone who has faith [Rom. 1:16]."

The actual content of salvation in the New Testament offers a wealth of meaning. The death of the Lord created present salvation for all with its liberation from law, sin and death (Rom. 6:1 ff; 1 Tim. 1:15; Eph. 2:1–10); God offers divine adoption (Rom. 8:14–17); grace justifies people (Rom. 3:24). Believers already experience the saving presence of God in their lives through Jesus even as they await the full expression of salvation (Heb. 9:28; Rom. 8:24; Phil. 3:20).[12]

The authors of the gospels present Jesus as the one who offered salvation. The angels proclaimed it to the shepherds (Lk. 2:30). Jesus himself extended it to all who would listen: the upright and the sinner, the rich and the poor. Each person had to make a personal commitment to the Lord as savior in order to experience the saving presence of God. Jesus broke the power of evil. Satan fell like lightning from heaven (Lk. 10:18). No longer might people think of history's outcome as either good or bad. Goodness is the only response. An irrevocable communion has been established between God and humankind. Evil and sin can never totally overcome the fundamental sense of goodness and unity that every human being has as a gift. Jesus as redeemer and savior offers the assurance that God and goodness have already triumphed. Peace and harmony and truth have become not only possible, but actual. The blind have seen; the lepers are cleansed; the lame walk; sinners have turned from their sins and people can walk in dignity because they have responded to Jesus as their personal savior. He offered not only a salvation for the future, but a present reality. The New Testament teems with references to what was accomplished within human lives. As savior he preserved them physically, psychologically and spiritually; he was a presence that healed mind and body and soul. He fulfilled Israel's expectations and longings for someone to restore the torn fabric of its covenantal history.

MEANING OF THE MODEL: SAVIOR

CONTEMPORARY enthusiasts turn quickly to Scripture and find in that record of revelation the fullest meaning of Jesus as personal savior. Throughout the gospels individuals come to Jesus and express their commitment to him in faith and thus experience his saving power. The same must be true today.

Evangelicals have long emphasized this model of Jesus. The history of Christianity in the United States demonstrates this concern. Traditionally, thousands of "born-again Christians" make their personal affirmation in faith after a moving presentation by a powerful preacher of God's word. Most Americans have witnessed, at least on television, the magnetism of Billy Graham. Many have participated in Protestant revival meetings or in the missions that used to be conducted regularly in American Roman Catholic parishes; these evoked a similar sense of repentance and commitment. Through these missions Roman Catholics often experienced a call to return from the ways of sin to receive the healing forgiveness of Jesus in the sacrament of penance. The parallel evangelical approach would have appealed to the sinner to change his or her way of living and make a permanent and personal commitment in faith to the saving presence of Jesus.

As savior, Jesus was concerned principally with the healing of the soul, the spiritual dimension of human life. Jesus saved people from sin and helped them to overcome their evil tendencies. Even when he did not always accomplish the total conquest of sin, a person believed that the savior would overlook individual failings, provided that the person had made a personal faith commitment. Jesus in his lifetime told people to sin no more; he continues to echo this same refrain throughout human history. It is the soul, the spirit that needs the saving presence of God. Jesus responded by giving people a sense of fulfillment in their spiritual lives. They could turn their backs on a life of sin and walk away from the darkness of evil into the light of goodness and truth. The evangelists preached the same theme, and it finds its expression in the charismatic movement today. Jesus continues to call his followers to make a basic commitment so that they can turn away from sin and become his holy people.

For many people who have become part of the charismatic movement, baptism in the Spirit initiates this spiritual moment.[18] People record how they have experienced the Spirit in a most intense and personal way through the instrumentality of others. While part of a prayer group, and often aware of personal resistance to the movement, the individual experiences a sense of God that he or she has never experienced before. All of a sudden the individual knows that his or her life has been affected by the presence of God through Jesus the savior and there can never be a return to a former way of living. Because of his born-again experience Charles Colson faced his prison term calmly and afterward decided to devote his life to the spreading of the gospel of Jesus. Renewed in the baptism of the Spirit, his life purpose became a testimony to the presence of Jesus as his savior, and the savior of all.

For others the experience of Jesus as personal savior has not been so foreign to a previous way of living. Many good Christians have experienced the baptism of the Spirit and found their Christian faith taking on an element that was previously lacking. They become enthusiastic about what they believe and grow in their personal commitment to the gospel message. Faith existed previously, but now it has been kindled to a new brightness. They begin to see everything in the light of the gospel and live accordingly. Again, often enough, these people were at first reluctant to get involved, but once part of the movement they too have become apostles who want to lead others to a similar commitment.

They have been healed in soul by the presence of Jesus as personal savior and will never again be the same.

The model of Jesus as savior does not stop at the healing of the soul. Jesus concerns himself with people and thus with the bodily aspects of human life as well. If Jesus is the personal savior, he must also be interested in the physical ills of his people, just as he was concerned with the physical needs of the people of his own time in Palestine. Thus, healing is closely associated with the charismatic movement.[14] The preacher will announce the presence of a sufferer with a particular malady and will declare that the illness is now cured. Or, an ill person will come to be healed through the laying on of hands by the leader or by the entire group. Scores of people have attested to healings through contact with the healer or through the ministry of a group of believers. Jesus as savior continues his healing ministry through the activity of the believing community. Once again, the lame walk, the blind see, the deaf hear—all through the power of Jesus present among his people. The savior promises and fulfills his promise.

When an individual believes in the power of Jesus as personal savior, then he can lay claim to the power of the resurrected Lord. This belongs to the Christian community by right—not because of anything they have done, but because of what Jesus has done for them. With such a claim, God will of necessity respond because God has so promised. Whatever is asked in the name of Jesus will be given. The enthusiasts will not excuse God from working miracles. Rather God must work miracles because God has bound himself to heal in Jesus his Son. The savior must be interested in the sufferings of his people and must help them. All the believer has to do is turn to the savior with complete confidence. Indeed, an incredible number of people seem to have been cured, and this has not been confined to what was once called the evangelical churches;

members of the Roman Catholic community as well as Lutherans, Episcopalians and others have charismatic leaders who bring the healing presence of the Lord to sick and troubled persons.

Finally, the experience of Jesus as personal savior also includes the healing of the psyche, the emotional and affective part of the human personality. Very often people need psychological healing, even more than spiritual or physical healing. In many instances the psyche prevents the person from knowing the saving presence of God, so it must be healed first. The savior concerns himself with how people feel and offers solace and comfort. People especially need the healing of memories. The contemporary charismatic movement has helped us appreciate that. People do not need to carry forever the burdens of their past.[15] They can experience the presence of their savior, whose presence heals the wounds inflicted by the past. People crippled emotionally need not continue in such a condition. The savior knows the needs of his followers and responds generously to those who have trust and faith in him.

As a result of the experience of Jesus as savior the believer will want to become an evangelist and lead others to experience the same saving presence of God in their lives. The contemporary experience shows a blurring of denominational lines among those who accept this model of Jesus. Whether one is a Roman Catholic or a Baptist or a Lutheran matters little. The faith dimension that has led an individual to know Jesus as Lord is everything. Many can be united into the one band of believers who have made their personal commitment to the Lord.

This enthusiasm also creates a powerful sense of community among believers. Christianity, no longer limited to Sunday observance, colors every aspect of a person's life. The Word of God becomes important as the vehicle for the Spirit and people become devoted to its expressions. Savior takes on a meaning that will be present in the ordinary details of human life and not restricted to the confines of textbooks.[16]

People who have accepted Jesus as savior find new meaning in their lives. Life is not absurd because the commitment to the Lord and the service of the brethren gives direction. The courage to live for others after experiencing the presence of God in Jesus gives a value and a purpose that cannot be adequately described unless the individual has experienced it. All people should live as Jesus lived, through the gift of the Spirit.

Believers are assured in the depth of their being that God holds their personal future and the future of the human race in his loving hands. No dark and mysterious force manipulates us. God's loving care controls our destiny and gives us the possibility of doing something with our lives.

There is no room here for a spirit of cynicism. Christians will never emphasize what is wrong or evil or bad or sinful; nor will they mock the presence of goodness. Christians are not the losers in life, but the ones who actually have achieved something of the peace and harmony that all desire. They have found themselves, for they have found their savior; they already experience benefits from his life even as they look forward to a better future.

The savior knows that we have failures, even when we have committed ourselves to him. The savior redeems us from all personal failure by telling his followers that in spite of our sin we have value in the eyes of God the Father. A new possibility exists. We can be more than we are at any one moment; we can always bring some sense of goodness to the fore and come closer to living the way that will bring peace. Even in the midst of personal failure the one who has been saved knows that he or she is still precious in the eyes of God, of Jesus and of his holy community. The one who has been saved knows no sense of isolation. Jesus is the friend who will never fail, the faithful one who will never be lacking in fidelity, even when people are unfaithful to him. The isolation and aloneness that often characterize human life find no place among those who have come to know Jesus as personal savior. They always have the Lord, and they always have around them other believers who have also experienced his saving presence. Jesus as savior redeems and saves his people with a richness often lost in words. Jesus saves his faithful ones from the power of evil and sin and gives them moments of peace. Far too many Christians experience each other as forces of damnation rather than of salvation. If people come to see and accept Jesus as their personal savior, the power of evil will be lessened in this world and in the lives of people. The savior will be the one who heals and restores, not only in theory but in fact.

ADVANTAGES

On a personal level, the advantages of this model are legion. Firstly, it is fully in accord with Scripture. Jesus came to heal people in mind and in body. He called for a change of heart and a change in living and promised to be with his followers and to give them the presence of his community. Everything that Jesus accomplished in the lives of his contemporaries he continues to fulfill in the world today. The model thus recaptures an understanding of Jesus found in Scripture and often overlooked in some of the theology and religious practices that have developed in the Christian tradition.

Salvation is concerned with the healing of the whole person, not just the soul. This model embraces the totality of the human being and relates the presence of God to that totality. Christianity as a religion is concerned not only with individuals' souls, but at the same time with the maladies of mind and body that mar that soul. The model relates Jesus to the many facets and

the many needs of human life and presents him as
someone who is concerned with all these facets.

The model depends on a personal commitment in
faith to the Lord. Many Christians belong to a Church
but never have made such a commitment. Just because
a person has grown up with Christianity does not necessarily mean that he or she has ever accepted Jesus. The
call for a commitment in faith to Jesus as personal savior emphasizes the role of individual faith as the foundation of Christianity. We cannot go through the mo-
tions of being committed to faith without the personal
relationship to the Lord.

The model also emphasizes the community aspect of
Christianity. Those who are committed to the Lord join
together in a life of fellowship and mutual care. Isolation and alienation should not be a part of Christianity.
Those who have come to believe in Jesus as personal
savior create a spirit of commitment to each other.
Groups of charismatics manifest a genuine concern for
each other that often astounds those outside the movement. The bond of faith in the Lord blossoms into a
sense of mutual love of the brethren which the gospel
of John claims as an essential characteristic of the
Christian community.

This model also has a definite effect on believers,
since they tend to become evangelists themselves—people who proclaim the good news of salvation to others.
These believers do not hide Christianity under a bushel
basket, but proclaim it from the rooftops. They become
enthusiastic preachers of the Lord, calling people to experience what they themselves have known. From a
small movement, the charismatic community in the
United States has quickly grown to include hundreds of
thousands throughout the world. The modern-day evangelists offer someone to believe in, someone who is concerned with every aspect of human life. They preach
and bring the good news to others with a sense of dedi-
cation that rivals that of the earliest preachers of the

gospel, and the most effective heralds of Christian history.

This model also contributes to a sense of well-being for the believer. If Jesus is my savior then there is nothing to be ashamed of in human life; no need to harbor the bad dreams of the past; belief banishes the sense of guilt that sometimes plagues every believer. Jesus has died and risen and has brought forgiveness and peace. No matter what a person may have done or failed to do, no matter what a person may do in the future, the savior never abandons his faithful ones. Sin can never destroy the fundamental sense of union that exists between the believer and Jesus:

> For I am sure that neither death nor life, nor angels, nor principalities, nor things present, nor things to come, nor powers, nor height, nor depth, nor anything else in all creation can separate us from the love of God which is in Christ Jesus [Rom. 8:38–39].

The commitment is too strong; the love of God too powerful. Such faith offers the believer no license to commit evil; rather, it helps an individual to rise from sin and failure without having to bear the damaging burden of guilt. The one who called sinners will always call sinners and will always offer forgiveness and peace. He does not hold grudges against people, but as savior he promises pardon to those who will turn to him in faith. Salvation is real for anyone who seeks it and accepts the offer.

This model also unites various Christian bodies in a unity of faith that has rarely been experienced in history. The denominational differences that have characterized the history of Christianity, especially during the last four hundred years, are not nearly so important as the bond of faith and love that should exist among people who have accepted Jesus as savior. The common bond of unity in Jesus creates a larger Christian com-

munity. The differences remain, but can never obliterate
the presence of Jesus as savior gathering his flock into
one fold.

The richness of this model can be seen in the lives of
those who have come to accept Jesus as Lord. People
seem dramatically changed; minds, bodies and souls are
healed; people are united with each other; lives become
more interesting; peace and harmony now characterize
the human story; Jesus is real in personal lives. No
wonder that so many have turned to this model of
Jesus.

LIMITATIONS

ALTHOUGH it is well in accord with Scripture, the model
does not embody the full picture of Jesus as presented
in the gospels and letters. Jesus the personal savior is
also the transcendent one; he is the Word of God made
flesh and experienced as savior, but he still remains the
Word of God, the eternal one, present with God (Jn.
1:1, 18). This savior did not work the miracles of
healing that would save all people from all ailments. He
raised Lazarus from the dead, but allowed him to die
again. The various images of Jesus from Scripture cannot easily be reduced to one approach.

This model, especially as evidenced in some of the
devotional expressions in the charismatic movement,
can tend to create an elitism in the Church. Historically, as Knox noted, the enthusiasts have tended to
separate themselves from anyone who did not agree
with them totally and have taken the stance that anyone
not like them falls short of the full living of Christianity
to which all are called. The enthusiast considers the exceptional experience of God the norm, the standard of
religious achievement. "He will have no almost Christians, no weaker brethren who plod and stumble."[17] A
sense of "holier than thou" can develop which, instead
of strengthening the presence of God in the community

and enhancing mutual love, can tend to divide and destroy.

In their devotion to the Word of God, enthusiasts sometimes tend to interpret the Word of God in the most fundamentalist sense. The Bible is accepted without limitations, even though it was written by limited human beings. The Bible can become a magic talisman —not only to give direction, but actually to plot the future and respond to all the questions of human life in a definite, clear and simple fashion. Scholarship is ignored as unnecessary or despised as unworthy of faith. Since the charismatic movement involves a broad cross-section of the Church, with a special appeal for those who are looking for clear answers, anyone who tries to present a different opinion on the Bible is sometimes seen as lacking in full faith or at least as dealing with issues which do not concern the true believer.

"Jesus as Savior" can so emphasize the relationship to Jesus that the whole sense of the Church as an organized community of believers falls into shadow. The sacraments, which are meant to be the outward expression of faith, are considered of minor consequence when compared to the baptism of the Spirit and other charismatic gifts. And while the ecumenical aspects of the model are heartening, it can lead to a false irenicism, if major doctrinal differences among the Christian churches are summarily dismissed.

Many have experienced the healing presence of God physically and emotionally as well as spiritually, but thousands of believers, many of them in the charismatic movement, seek a healing of mind and body and do not experience it. Is this due to a lack of faith? What of the suffering of the innocent? If Jesus as savior can perform miracles, is he not discriminating against those he does not heal? Even those who seem most faithful to him experience painful deaths, which seems out of character for his goodness.[18] Does the model deal sufficiently with the power of evil and sin and suffering in life, or are there other components that have been overlooked?

A paradigm responds to more questions than an ordinary model; it allows for greater development of possibilities. According to this standard, the model of Jesus as savior cannot be the paradigm we are seeking, for too many important issues remain unanswered—not the least of which is the question of human suffering.

The sense of prayer, the commitment of the people to the Lord Jesus, can never be gainsaid. Historically, we know that the enthusiastic movements flourished at different periods, often in reaction to the rigidity in Christianity and sometimes because of the lack of attention paid to the role of faith. With the passing of time, the groups often became more rigid than what they rebelled against; they tended to cast into shadow certain fundamental elements of Christianity while they stressed others.

The sobering remarks of Ronald Knox should be recalled, however, at the end of this chapter as well as at the beginning:

> Where wealth abounds, it is easy to mistake shadow for substance; the fires of spirituality may burn low and we go on unconscious, dazzled by the glare of tinsel suns.[19]

Because of enthusiasm, inertia is not only a vice but a virtue. We must trust all to the kindness of a loving savior. That is the virtue. However, we cannot run from the world, refusing to recognize its problems and what we can do to solve some of them. That is the vice. How difficult to unravel the two!

NOTES

1. The 1979 Eastern Conference in New York, September 21–23.
2. Publicity used for the Eastern General Conference.

3. R. Knox, *Enthusiasm* (New York: Oxford University Press, 1949). See Larry Christenson, *A Message to the Charismatic Movement* (Minneapolis: Division, 1972). This author compares the Catholic Apostolic Church of the late nineteenth century to the present movement and sees the former as a forerunner of the latter.

4. Knox, p. 1.

5. *Ibid.*, p. 2.

6. *Ibid.*, p. 4.

7. *Ibid.*, p. 591.

8. *Ibid.*

9. See O'Grady, *Jesus, Lord and Christ,* Chapter 6.

10. See "Redemption," *Dictionary of the Bible,* John L. McKenzie (Milwaukee: Bruce, 1965).

11. See B. Willems, *The Reality of the Redemption* (New York: Herder and Herder, 1970), pp. 49–60.

12. O'Grady, *Jesus, Lord and Christ,* pp. 74–75.

13. See S. Clark, *Baptized in the Spirit* (Pecos, N.M., 1970); S. Tugwell, *Did You Receive the Spirit?* (New York: Paulist, 1972); G. Montague, *The Spirit and His Gifts* (New York, 1974); J. Dunn, *Baptism in the Holy Spirit* (London: SCM Press, 1970); E. Jorstad, ed., *The Holy Spirit in Today's Church* (New York: Abingdon, 1973). Jorstad gives an excellent summary in Chapter 6, pp. 58–76.

14. See René Laurentin, *Catholic Pentecostals* (New York: Doubleday, 1977), pp. 100–31. Also, Jorstad, Chapter 8, pp. 100–18. Jorstad also has an excellent section on demonology.

15. See E. O'Connor, *The Pentecostal Movement in the Catholic Church* (South Bend: Notre Dame Press, 1971) and Laurentin, pp. 115–16. See also J. Gunstone, *Greater Things Than These* (New York: Faith Press, 1974), pp. 64–65.

16. O'Grady, *Jesus, Lord and Christ,* pp. 77–80.

17. Knox, *Enthusiasm,* p. 2.

18. Cf. H. Nouwen, *In Memoriam* (Notre Dame: Ave Maria, 1979).

19. Knox, p. 591.

8

THE SEARCH FOR A
BIBLICAL CHRISTOLOGY

THROUGHOUT THE PREVIOUS chapters I referred frequently to the New Testament as a basis for the models or to indicate the lack of support that a particular model of Jesus might find among the authors of the New Testament. Actually, the New Testament will give support for all of the models treated if the reader carefully selects the authors and quotations.

Christology seeks to offer a systematic presentation of the meaning of Jesus of Nazareth. Concerned with the human effort to understand faith in Jesus, the writers of the New Testament gathered together many strands into a unified whole. In the past, many authors have attempted to construct a Christology founded on the New Testament. Such a claim, however, often demonstrates little knowledge of the various theological traditions. The New Testament contains many Christologies of many different authors coming from diverse communities—all making a just claim to offer some true insights into Jesus of Nazareth.

The Bible is the gospel of the living God, since in reading it we hear God's voice. It is not primarily doctrine or a grouping of articles of faith, but a record of a conscious religious life lived by the Jewish people and by Jesus and his followers. We will understand it not through some historical-critical method alone, but only by actually living out the faith that is its source and direction.

The New Testament documents the faith of the members of the Christian community after they had the experience of the risen Lord, and believed in him as the messiah in power (Rom. 1:4). When we read the Bible we become aware of the experience of Jesus and the faith of the early followers, but what we read is the record of that faith and not the faith itself. The New Testament shares in the mystery of God and the mystery of human life, which means that we can reach some understanding but can never reach complete clarity. The mystery does not imply that we know nothing, but it does mean that we will never know everything. If we can never reach a complete understanding of ourselves, how can we expect to understand the mystery that is Jesus of Nazareth?

Although we rely on the presence of God's Spirit in the Church, our source for the life and the meaning of Jesus is the record left by writers some two thousand years ago and this makes our task all the more difficult. If we cannot reach a complete understanding of Jesus today, the same thing holds for any believer or group of believers at any period of history. Even those who were privileged to know Jesus and to live with him and learn from him were limited in their appreciation of him. Thus we cannot expect to develop a complete, accurate and systematic Christology even from the earliest documents of Christianity. The New Testament authors display neither harmony in their sayings about Jesus nor a sense of a unified doctrinal approach to him. These documents come from a specific time and place; they are human, with all of the defects and limitations of any human accomplishment. We can certainly gain much from a study of the New Testament in our search for Christology, but that includes a careful awareness of the historical ambit, the social and cultural and religious milieu of Jesus' time and place. As we study, we may well end up knowing less than what we presumed at the outset.

God chose to act with people in a human way; thus the gospels would have to be limited and expressed within certain spiritual ideas common to all people. The Word was made flesh, but not flesh in general. Jesus was a man, a Jew born in a specific era in a particular country. What he did and what he taught have been expressed in human terms taken from that time and that region, and thus part of the heritage of Judaism.

The first preachers of Jesus also lived within the confines of a particular education and culture. When Jesus spoke of God he did so in terms of his own understanding of God, and his listeners understood him in terms of their own perceptions. If he spoke of Father, the listeners formulated their image of father according to their own lights. And so the Christology of the New Testament is limited by the people and events that surrounded Jesus of Nazareth, as well as by the limitations of the earliest preachers.

Each author of the gospels understood Jesus within a certain harmony and unity of viewpoints. They compared their appreciation of Jesus as risen Lord to what they had known before and integrated this new experience with their own understanding of human personality, and formulated it in their own way and with their own categories. All of this resulted in a great diversity in the New Testament images of Jesus. The only honest approach to biblical Christology is to admit that no one biblical Christology exists; there are as many Christologies as there are authors and communities that tried to express in writing something of their experience of Jesus. Even individual writers can offer an early Christology and a later Christology. Paul, for example, presents a slightly different understanding of Jesus in his earlier epistles than in the later ones. The gospels give evidence of several Christologies in the community, along with a contest as to the superiority of one over the other.

I cannot hope to present in this short chapter a detailed presentation of the various Christologies of the New Testament. An overview, however, is possible and helpful in this effort to study the models of Jesus.

THE EARLIEST CHRISTOLOGICAL FORMULA[1]

THE New Testament evidences a certain natural evolution in the understanding of Jesus. Since the writings in the New Testament are collections of pericopes elaborated over a period of time, the reader cannot easily detect precisely what the primitive Church preached. For example, Acts 3:12–26, 4:9–12 and 5:30–32 seem to be primitive and to date from the time immediately after Pentecost; today scholars generally admit that even they have been theologically elaborated.

> The God of our Fathers raised Jesus whom you killed by hanging him on a tree. God exalted him at his right hand as Leader and Savior, to give repentance to Israel and forgiveness of sins. (Acts 5:30–31)

Authors will not even agree on the primitiveness of "Maranatha" (Come, Lord Jesus, or May the Lord Jesus come). Some authors construct ancient formulas from Matthew 25:31–46, Mark 14:61 and Luke 12:8.

> And I tell you, everyone who acknowledges me before men, the Son of Man also will acknowledge before the angels of God. (Lk. 12:8)

These seem to have come from a Palestinian milieu, which would suggest a more ancient origin, but the theory still has serious drawbacks.

The chief stumbling block is the question of the *Parousia*. Was the *Parousia* part of the earliest testimony of Jesus or not? Some maintain that the most ancient Judaic-Christian Christology contained a theology of exaltation without a second coming. Jesus after his death was raised by God and was justified and as such now lives with God; another coming in glory was not expected; the eschatological time of salvation exists now, as proven by the outpouring of the Spirit.

A second opinion maintains that the Christian community expected a second and definitive coming of the Lord. Therefore they did not consider the exaltation as full nor the institution of Jesus in power as complete. Christ was taken for a time, and only in his second coming will he be instituted as messiah in the sense of the Son of Man in Daniel (Dan. 7:13–14). It is in this light that they would interpret Acts 3:20–21: "and that he might send the Christ, appointed for you, Jesus, whom heaven must receive until the time for establishing all that God spoke by the mouth of his holy prophets . . ."

Certainly the earliest Christologies were formulas of exaltation. Jesus was exalted, raised up in power (Rom. 1:4; Acts 2:36), and since the Spirit was actually given, perhaps there was no need for a further exaltation in a second coming. But since the Jews expected a glorious messiah, a role Jesus did not fulfill, in all probability the thought of a *Parousia* was soon added to this earliest Christological formula. Without a second coming in glory it would be difficult for Jews to accept a crucified messiah.

The advantage of an exaltation Christology without a second coming is that it accentuates the salvation already present among the followers of Jesus. This gives the foundation for a realized eschatology which the New Testament will develop at a later stage. The *Parousia* adds the future element to salvation and gives the foundation for what has come to be known as traditional eschatology.

EVOLUTION IN THE NEW TESTAMENT

THE New Testament also allows us to chart a development in the Church's understanding of the divinity of Jesus.[2] The earliest formulation in the *kerygma* emphasized that Jesus was made messiah in his resurrection (Acts 2:36). Thinking would have centered on Jesus becoming the Son of God in the experience of his resurrection. The Father raised Jesus up as a final testimony of his acceptance of the life and death of his faithful Son, and by this means Jesus was made Lord and messiah.

At this point there might have been a further development into the future with the advent of the *Parousia*. For some, this would be the final manifestation of the favor of God on Jesus his Son. Jesus would become Lord and messiah in the fullest sense in his second coming. Later thinking on the ministry of Jesus encouraged seeing Jesus as already the messiah in his activity and in his preaching. In the gospel of Mark the baptism begins his ministry (Mk. 1:11). Since he fulfilled the expectations of Israel in his ministry he was God's favored Son in his baptism. Later theologians would falsely interpret this scene in the light of an adoptionist Christology: the Father adopted Jesus as beloved Son in his baptism.

Still further thought situated Jesus as God's unique Son, not only in his ministry but from his very conception. Matthew and Luke offer infancy stories which present the virginal conception as the sign of the unique Sonship of Jesus.

Finally, the Logos theology of John identifies Jesus with the preexistent Word of God, the one who exists in the form of God (Jn. 1:1). This highest Christology of the later writings of the New Testament concludes the natural evolution in thought that began with an experience of Jesus. The New Testament does not attempt to relate all of these ideas; it shares no great concern to explain how Jesus was divine and human. Rather, it simply presents from a variety of viewpoints the attestation in faith of the uniqueness of Jesus as Son and one like us in all things but sin (Heb. 4:15).

THE CHRISTOLOGY OF THE GOSPELS

A STUDY of the different gospels will demonstrate the clear distinctions that existed in the early community. Each author's perspective flowed from the needs of his particular audience. Each presents a Christology that is not meant to be exclusive or exhaustive. Only when the richness of this variety of approaches to Jesus is understood can we begin to appreciate the impact that Jesus had on people.

1. Mark

The gospel of Mark[3] has no infancy narrative and appears to locate Jesus' divine Sonship in his baptism. If we examine the gospel more closely, however, it becomes evident that, for Mark, Jesus is first and foremost the suffering Son of Man who must die. On three occasions Mark has Jesus give a prediction of his passion: Mark 8:31, 9:31 and 10:33–34. The general theology that pervades the gospel of Mark focuses on the fate of those who are faithful to God. They hear the Word of God and preach it, they are rejected and are delivered up. John the Baptist preaches and he is delivered up (1:14); Jesus preaches and is delivered up (9:30; 10:33); the disciples preach and they too are delivered up (13:9). Death appears to be the fate of all.

In order to understand the Christology of Mark, we must first appreciate his fundamental Christian anthropology. Whatever happens to Jesus will also happen to his followers. It is a sad gospel in many ways, filled with misunderstandings on the part of the disciples, and with pain inflicted on Jesus as he is abandoned by family and friends and eventually by the entire population. Mark wishes to speak about Jesus, but only in relationship to the sufferings that are part of the Christian experience. Jesus as the suffering Son of Man is the model for all who would be disciples.

However central the death of Jesus is to Mark's gospel, it is not his sole concern. He is also concerned about how Jesus lived. In presenting Jesus' way of suffering and his rejection, Mark always places it within the context of the life of Jesus as one who serves. The climax of his teaching on suffering thus includes his way of living: "The Son of Man came not to be served but to serve and to give his life as a ransom for many [Mk. 10:45]." The author presents the cross not so much as an atonement for sin, but as the result of obedience to the law of God in life. God mysteriously wills that his Son must suffer and die, so the Son willingly accepts his fate (Mk. 8:31: "the Son of man *must* suffer . . ."). Jesus is patterned after the righteous sufferer in Psalm 22:

My God, my God why has thou abandoned me . . .
Yet thou are holy, enthroned on the praises of Israel,
Yet thou are he who took me from the womb, thou
*   didst keep me safe upon my mother's breast.*
Be not far from me for trouble is near and there is
*   none to help.* (Ps. 22:1, 3, 9, 11)

Jesus is the model for others in his living and dying, but his actual death offers the deepest insight into Mark's Christology. The death of Jesus on the cross lays open a quality of life which patterns what true life means for all people. The authentic follower of Jesus must take up the cross daily and follow the Lord. No optional road, no substitute and no other means exist by which a person can be a disciple. Mark brings his Christology into the closest possible contact with the

Church and the individual believer, and in so doing he reveals the incarnational Christology that will pervade his gospel. Mark presents in his gospel an apocalyptic drama in which the author and his community are self-consciously caught up in events they view as the end of history. The gospel portrays this drama in the three acts previously mentioned: John is delivered up (1:14); Jesus is delivered up (9:31; 10:33; 14:41) and finally the Christian is delivered up (13:9–13). The conclusion, however, should not be forgotten. The believers are sad as they experience persecution, but they are also filled with the hope directed toward sharing in the glorification of the Son of Man. For Mark, the cross and suffering stand always in the foreground, but the resurrection remains in the background as the foundation for hope. As the Son of Man must suffer and die and then rise, so he offers the same hope to those who will follow him. The glorified Lord will bring his faithful followers to share in his glory. Mark understood Jesus only in terms of the suffering messiah who asks his disciples to join with him and share in his sufferings so that all can share in his glory.

The gospel of Mark is not the happiest of gospels. The shadow of the cross hangs over the life of Jesus as it will hang over the lives of his followers. The false Christology of a divine man who experiences glory is corrected by the true Christology that involves a sharing of his sufferings. To a persecuted community, Mark offered consolation by reminding them that all who will follow a thorn-crowned Lord must expect to share in his pain before they can enter into his glory.

2. Luke

The gospel of Luke[4] presents an entirely different picture of Jesus. No longer Mark's suffering Son of Man, Jesus is seen here as the perfect Greek gentleman: filled with the Spirit of God and endowed with the gift of effectively preaching the Word of God. Jesus' appearance in the synagogue in Nazareth early in Luke's gospel sets the tone for what follows. Jesus as the teacher is invested with the power of the Spirit. He fulfills in himself the prophecy of Isaiah: "The spirit of the Lord is upon me . . . today this scripture is fulfilled in your hearing" (Lk. 4:18, 21). In his ministry people are impressed by his authority (4:31, 36–37). He shows his power in his deeds, for he is not only the messenger of the kingdom, but also its messianic agent who reveals the eschatological reign of God through how he acts. This confluence of word and deed gives him power over the forces of evil. Thus he banishes Satan in the course of his ministry (4:39) and subjects evil spirits to himself (4:36); he cures by his word (4:39) and in his role as the teacher he heals (5:17–26; 6:6–11).

Luke's is a gospel of great joy. Jesus brings blessedness to all who respond to him in faith. At his birth the angels proclaim a message of joy for all (2:11); Jesus rejoices at the return of his disciples from preaching (10:20) and rejoices over one sinner who repents (15:10).

The Christology of Luke captures the mercy and compassion of Jesus. His fifteenth chapter is often called "the gospel within the gospel" for in it Luke presents three central parables: the lost sheep, the lost coin and the prodigal son. In each instance the story illustrates the mercy and forgiveness of God and the joy over a sinner who repents and returns. His compassion extends to the outcasts of society calling them to be his friends. Shepherds, outcasts themselves, welcomed him at his birth. The same pattern continues throughout his ministry. Sinners are always welcome; tax collectors, prostitutes and anyone else who feels left out can find company with Jesus as the forgiving savior.

Luke also portrays Jesus as a great man of prayer. He prayed just before his baptism (3:21); after he worked miracles he withdrew to pray (5:16); he prayed all night before choosing his disciples (6:12);

he prayed after the miracle of the loaves (9:18); he prayed as a prelude to the transfiguration (9:28–29); he was praying when his disciples asked him to teach them to pray (11:1); and he prayed in the garden (22:39–45) and from the cross (23:46). For Luke, Jesus always remains in close contact with God.

Jesus has a universal interest in this gospel. In his prayer Simeon joins together Israel and the pagan world as recipients of the salvation that Jesus brings (2:31–32). Jesus in Luke calls a Roman centurion and a Samaritan leper models of faith (7:9; 17:19). Luke also emphasizes the concern of Jesus for women. Jesus treats women with a special compassion. He heals the woman with a hemorrhage (8:43–48); cares for a woman who is a sinner (7:36–50); responds to the need of the widow of Naim (6:11–17) and women provide for him (23:55).

This same gospel deals with the special relationship that existed between Jesus and God his Father. He is the Son of God (3:22; 22:29; 24:49) and, like Matthew, Luke has his version of the so-called Johannine thunderbolt in the synoptic tradition:

> *Everything has been given to me by my Father. No one knows the Son except the Father and no one knows the Father except the Son and anyone to whom the Son wishes to reveal him.* (Lk. 10:22)

At his baptism God declared him to be his Son, but previously in the infancy narrative his very conception was an act of God, making him the Son of the Most High (1:32). The Father who gives Jesus his mission of salvation has decreed all (22:22) and has given Jesus the Spirit to fulfill this mission. Finally, after Jesus has been raised up by the Father, he too can send the Spirit (24:49 ff, Acts 1:1 ff).

Luke presents Jesus as the Spirit-filled prophet who manifests the designs of God for the salvation of all; the kind and compassionate Jesus prays much and expects his followers to do likewise. In all of his ministry, God his Father directs him as he proclaims the inbreaking of the kingdom of God and announces the end of the power of evil. In the Acts of the Apostles, the continuation of Luke's gospel, we learn of the continuing presence of this saving Lord in the Church. He remains with his people always.

3. Matthew

Matthew[5] begins his gospel by carefully presenting Jesus as both Son of David and Son of Abraham (Mt. 1:1); the one foretold of old now fulfills all of the expectations of Israel; in him all of the nations of the world are blessed. Jesus stands in this gospel as a great authoritative and ethical teacher; he is part of the tradition of Israel. Like the great leader, Moses, Jesus gives clear guidance and direction to his people. He inaugurates the kingdom of God and, as the final agent and plenipotentiary, he consummates God's purpose in the world (Mt. 5:17–18). Jesus in Matthew's gospel is the founder of the New Israel, the Church which brings to fulfillment all of the ancient expectations. Matthew has a peculiar interest in the Old Testament and frequently refers to Old Testament prophecies that are accomplished in Jesus. In the infancy narrative alone, five times he refers to the law and uses the passages to demonstrate that Jesus fulfills Israel's hopes foretold by the prophets.

As teacher Jesus' authority commanded respect in Mark (1:27) but Matthew is more interested in giving the content of this teaching in the sermon on the mountain (5:1–7:29). Matthew is concerned in systematizing the teaching of Jesus into a unified body. This tendency agrees with the general tone of the gospel, which presents a community that is clearly organized. The author tries, in fact, to present as orderly a teaching on ethics as can be found in the Old Testament (Deuteronomy and Leviticus).

Apologetical overtones are heard throughout the gospel, especially in the infancy narratives and in the passion account. These two sections would have been of special interest to Jewish converts, and so Matthew relates the experiences of Jesus in both instances to the Old Testament. He demonstrates that in truth Jesus is the messiah of Israel, and offers explanations that he hopes will convince his readers that the messiah had to suffer.

Following the general pattern developed in the other Synoptics, Matthew presents the fundamental messiahship of Jesus but nuances its meaning. He alone among the Synoptics adds to Peter's confession of Jesus as the messiah "The Son of the living God [Mt. 16:16]." He alone gives the injunction against the sword at the time of Jesus' arrest, which indicates for him that Jesus was not the political figure of popular messianic expectation (26:52).

Matthew also deals with the theme of the suffering servant (as does Mark) but has a distinctive way of portraying this element of his Christology. Mark interprets Jesus' mission in light of the suffering servant by subtle overtones while Matthew actually identifies Jesus with this figure from Deutero-Isaiah. The author of Matthew's gospel seems to perceive more deeply the mission of Jesus to be the servant of all and to bear the suffering of his passion and death for the sake of the many.

More so than in any of the other gospels, Jesus is Lord for Matthew. Even when Satan approaches in the temptation narrative he does so with the reverence due the Lord. A sense of adoration pervades his ministry, from the adoration of the Magi to Peter falling down and confessing his belief in Jesus as Lord (2:11; 14:33). That Jesus is the Son of God in a most unusual way, Matthew demonstrates in the story of his origin and exemplifies in his ministry. He has authority and power and commands a sense of awe and adoration. As

the Lord, he teaches with authority and gives specific
directions to all who will come after him. Finally, as the
eschatological Lord, Jesus lives in his church until the
end of time (28:17–20).

The Christology of Matthew develops further insights
into the meaning of Jesus by presenting him not only as
the fulfillment of the Old Law but especially as the divine lawgiver, the exalted Lord, worthy of worship,
present always in the Church. He suffers, but his suffering pales in light of the meaning of his Lordship.

4. John

The figure of Jesus in the Fourth Gospel is central. His
work and his person form the heart of the gospel,
which becomes intelligible only when one has mas-
tered the meaning of Johannine Christology. Like the
other gospels, John[6] has his distinctive approach. In
the past, many scholars have searched for the hermeneutical key to Johannine Christology that would
help in understanding the entire gospel. They studied
the titles; they explored the relationship between the human and the divine, history and faith, person and function—but they never agreed on a single key. One possible approach, which I favor, focuses on relating Christology to anthropology.

John clearly emphasizes the divinity of Jesus. He begins his gospel with a hymn to the Word which relates
the eternal Word to the historical Jesus (Jn. 1:13).
The theology of the prologue relates this Word not only
to the incarnation and to God, but also to the meaning
of creation and to the response expected from those
who hear this Word (1:12). Along with this sense of
divinity comes the awareness that the divine finds resolution in a human response. Then the meaning of Jesus
is complete.

The title Son of Man also figures prominently in the
Fourth Gospel. This implies an appreciation of the divinity of Jesus because for John, unlike the Synoptics

who stress the suffering Son of Man and his future exaltation, the title connotes his preexistence and his glorification (2:13–15). Jesus uses this title in the gospel and implies that he is more than just an ordinary human being.

But this title "Son of Man" can also mean "everyman." A preexistent and glorified Son of Man exists, but this divine being lives in human history and bears the mark of "everyman." As was true for the Logos title, so also the Son of Man calls for a sense of commitment to him: "Do you believe in the Son of Man?" (10:35). The twofold understanding of humanity and divinity finds its full expression in the faith experience of a believer.

John has a characteristic use of *ego eimi* (I am). The phrase recalls the use of the words in Deutero-Isaiah (e.g., 41:4; 43:10; 46:4) and can substitute for the holy name of God. Once again John emphasizes Jesus' divinity but also recalls his humanity, for he uses the expression as a predicate as well: Jesus says, I am the way, the truth, the light, the vine, the good shepherd, the door, the bread. The ordinary aspects of life disclose the divine presence. God the Father, through Jesus, calls all to come to the light, eat the bread, remain united to the vine.

Jesus is also preeminently Son in this gospel, where the close relationship that exists between Jesus and the Father is constantly emphasized; but he is also the son of Joseph (1:45). As Son, Jesus calls people to believe in him, to recognize him as the presence of the Father (14:9).

New Testament Christology reaches its highest development in the gospel of John. Jesus, the preexistent Word, always speaks from eternity; he knows the secrets of people's hearts; knows all that will happen to him and yet allows the drama to be played out. Jesus is divine in this gospel, not only in his baptism, his resurrection and his birth, but prior to all these events. He was with God and, as Word, was God.

Further examination of the relationship of the human and divine in this gospel, as well as a study of the relationship of faith and history and the question of function and person, demonstrates that Johannine Christology presents a distinct advance on the meaning of Jesus of Nazareth. The early Church has progressed considerably from the earliest formulation. At the same time the gospel does not lose sight of the origins of Christology: Jesus is still human and always calls people to faith.

The theologies of Paul and the other writers of the New Testament present their own peculiar approaches to Jesus as well. Each offers different nuances to continue the process of unfathoming the mystery of Jesus. Our study shows no single Christology in the New Testament; rather, there are as many Christologies as there are authors who try to enter into the mystery of Jesus. To be faithful to the New Testament demands a broad approach to Jesus that will not limit the presentation to any one of the gospels or any one single strand of a single gospel, but will rather recognize that the diversity is part of the treasure that has become the legacy of Christianity.

If we find it impossible to understand the mystery of one single human life, then how much more difficult it must be to unravel the meaning of Jesus in one way to the exclusion of all others. In Jesus we deal with the mystery of both the human and the divine.

When we examine each gospel and the scholarship it has generated, we discover that many different interpretations exist, coming from different scholars over the centuries. Some will study the Christology of one writer in the New Testament and overlook another, or will emphasize one idea to the exclusion of another. When we multiply this effort by four and then include the various approaches to the epistles, the task exceeds comprehension. To present one systematic Christology of the New Testament would be helpful, but it is an impossible task. We have always only the human effort to enter into the mystery of Jesus and present it in a limited fashion so that succeeding generations might benefit from the experience of others. No one biblical Christology exists; the believer and the Church find only human efforts to come to some personal or communal appreciation of the meaning of Jesus. With this foundation, we can return to the search for a paradigm and evaluate the entire process as well as the individual models we have examined. No matter what conclusions we reach, however, the result will always be tempered by the thought that the New Testament is richer in its Christology than any paradigm.

NOTES

1. See R. Fuller, *Foundations of New Testament Christology* (New York: Scribner's, 1965), pp. 143–73; J.A.T. Robinson, "The Most Primitive Christology of All," *Journal of Theological Studies*, vol. 7 (1956), pp. 177–89; D. Stanley, "The Primitive Preaching," *Concilium*, vol. 2 (1966), pp. 47–52.

2. See R. Brown, *The Birth of the Messiah* (New York: Doubleday, 1977), pp. 29–32.

3. W. Carroll, "The Jesus of Mark's Gospel," *Bible Today*, #103 (1979), pp. 2105–12; J. Donahue, "Jesus as the Parable of God in the Gospel of Mark," *Interpretation*, 32 (1978), pp. 369–86; T. Weeden, *Traditions in Conflict* (Philadelphia: Fortress, 1971); W. Harrington, "The Gospel of Mark: A Theologia Crucis," *Doctrine and Life*, vol. 26 (1976), pp. 24–33; J. Lambrecht, "The Christology of Mark," *Biblical Theology Bulletin*, 3 (1973), pp. 256–73.

4. See O. Betz, "The Kerygma of Luke," *Interpretation*, vol. 22 (1968), pp. 131–46; D. Jones, "The Title 'Christos' in Luke–Acts," *New Testament Studies*, vol. 18 (1971–72), pp. 39–53; C. Talbert, "An Anti-Gnostic Tendency in Lukan Christology," *New Testament Studies*, vol. 14 (1967–68), pp. 259–71.

5. See E. Gaston, "The Messiah of Israel as Teacher of the Gentiles," *Interpretation*, vol. 29 (1975), pp. 24–40; M. Johnson, "Reflections on a Wisdom Approach to Matthew's Christology," *Catholic Biblical Quarterly*, vol. 36 (1974), pp. 44–64; J. Kingsbury, *Matthew: Structure, Christology, Kingdom* (Philadelphia: Fortress, 1975); J. Meier, *The Vision of Matthew* (New York: Paulist, 1979); M. Suggs, *Wisdom, Christology and Law in Matthew's Gospel* (Cambridge: Harvard University Press, 1970).

6. See J. Giblet, "The Johannine Theology of the Logos," *The Word* (New York: Kenedy, 1964), pp. 104–46; M. Boismard, "Jesus the Savior According to John," *Word and Mystery* (Westminster: Newman, 1968), pp. 69–86; R. Collins, "The Representative Figures of the Fourth Gospel," *Downside Review*, vol. 94 (1976), pp. 26–46, 118–32; R. Fortna, "Christology in the Fourth Gospel: Redaction-Critical Perspectives," *New Testament Studies*, vol. 21 (1975), pp. 489–504; P. Harner, *The "I Am" of the Fourth Gospel* (Philadelphia: Fortress, 1970).

EVALUATING THE MODELS

THE PREVIOUS CHAPTERS have involved a certain dialectic. Many models exist and each one has both advantages and disadvantages. All have arisen in Christian history and all claim to have their basis in a close analysis of Scripture, but each one has come from a different tradition, from believers who have had different horizons within which they have chosen to judge the suitability of their model. A question that must have arisen as the reader progressed through the various models is: Which ones are compatible, not only with each other, but with the general consensus of Christianity as it has been manifested through the centuries? Are the different perspectives and conclusions mutually exclusive or are they complementary? Can anyone state with certainty that one model far surpasses another? Must we be content with admitting that each model is equally good and valuable without any attempt to evaluate them in the light of their distinctive advantages and disadvantages? The more important question might be: Is each model a help or a hindrance to the understanding of Jesus? Are they relatively opaque, so as to reduce the reality of Jesus to only a glimmer of light, or are they translucent—not so clear as to permit perfect visibility, but still giving a good view of the reality to all those who will use them?

The choice of any model will always depend upon

certain criteria, but who is to establish the criteria? For anyone to set up a number of criteria can in itself be a choice of values. The person who writes a book filled with personal ideas and then sets out to discover some support for the theories presented is like the theologian who chooses a model and then sets out to establish the criteria that will support the choice. Theologians who read the New Testament seeking to find support for a particular model of Jesus may assiduously overlook any themes that seem to support a conflicting model, or at least a different one.

Certainly the model should be clear and should account for the divinity of Jesus, but it should also respect his humanity. It should be mystical as well as practical. It should be subjective, since that is how we learn, but objective, too, since that will hold us to a firm basis in fact and reality. The model should relate to the experience of the poor, since the Church must identify with the poor if it is to be true to the example of Jesus. Founded always on the New Testament, any model should be appreciated and understood in the history of the Church and in the history of theology. If it could be final and definitive, then it would give a firm basis for faith; but it should also be provisional, since the understanding of faith is always developing. How can these paradoxes be resolved?

The spectrum of criteria cannot be reduced to internal considerations of theology, but must cover, as well, personal piety, official Church teaching, various Christian traditions, the fears and anxieties of those who shy away from examining certain of the models, and a host of other hidden agenda.

In any effort to evaluate, the one making the study must be aware of the tendency to emphasize one over the other, or to emphasize the extremes in every position other than the one proposed. A sincere desire to progress in understanding Jesus precludes the choice of criteria that will support only one model over the others. A number of criteria should already have become evident in the examination of the models in the individual chapters above. Let us now consider seven:

1. A firm basis in Scripture. In the return to the Bible by all Christian traditions as the authentic presentation of the Word of God, there has developed a sense of confidence in being on the right track if we can find a firm basis for our theology in the Scripture. If we are to deal with the models of Jesus, then the principal support must come from the New Testament.

2. Compatibility with Christian tradition. Christians have understood the Bible in their own historical situation. They have struggled with the question of Jesus and have offered many different answers to the questions that have arisen over the centuries. Since we are concerned with an image that can be accepted as a model and perhaps even as a paradigm, it must respond to many of the facets of Christian understanding of Jesus. We are not interested in returning to ancient Palestine, but are concerned rather with the relationship of the century of Jesus' birth to the succeeding nineteen.

3. A capacity to help Christians in their efforts to believe in Jesus. Believers do not live in a vacuum. Christians living in the twentieth century need a model that will help them to relate to a world quite different from anything that has preceded it. Developments in science, an awareness of the religious, philosophical and ethnic pluralism in this world, a wider appreciation of religion —all of these will have an effect on the model of Jesus. After experiencing so much world tragedy, the Christian needs a model that will speak eloquently to the heart that seeks to believe.

4. A capacity to direct believers to fulfill their mission as members of the Church. A model of Jesus unrelated to the activity of the Church in the world is not faithful to the Jesus of the gospels. Every gift con-

tains a corresponding responsibility, so the model that impels believers to live their Christian heritage must be favored.

5. Correspondence with the Christian religious experience today. Ever since Cardinal Newman wrote *On Consulting the Faithful in Matters of Dogma* we have been troubled by its implications. It has always been the tradition of the Church to pay attention to the lived beliefs of Christians in matters of faith, but the Church has used this cautiously. To take the principle seriously means that we must be concerned with the model of Jesus that good-living believers actually use today. We are not concerned with theological subtlety, but rather the faith experience of the masses of Christians. How do people view Jesus in their personal lives?

6. Theological fruitfulness. We have noted the strengths and weaknesses of the models and their relationship to theology. Old models have given way to new models, some advancing the theological enterprise, others hindering it. The model that can provide solutions for more of the theological questions that are being raised, and that offers the potential for more development, must be considered of greater value.

7. The ability to foster a good sense of Christian anthropology. Christology always involves an anthropology: the more we understand ourselves, the more we can understand Jesus, and vice versa. If a model can help Christians in coming to better sense of the meaning of Christianity as actually lived by people, if it can help define such a thing as the Christian self-image, then it is clearly of considerable value.

To evaluate six models by all seven criteria would be tedious. I have already given some indications in the individual chapters of the strengths and weaknesses of each model, and no doubt some readers have already made their decision on the model that best will serve them as a paradigm. The following summary of possible conclusions may be helpful in reaching a decision or evaluating a decision already reached.

The model of Jesus as Second Person of the Blessed Trinity has a weak basis in Scripture, but a much stronger one in tradition. It has little direct relation to fostering personal faith, since it seems divorced from people's ordinary lives. It also tends to encourage the split between the sacred and the secular, since it emphasizes the Church over the marketplace. It corresponds to the religious experience of many believers, but often only superficially, based more on a lack of alternatives than felt conviction. It has been theologically fruitful, since it has dominated the theology of the Church, spiritual theology, and has been the backdrop for objective moral theology, but it has not been helpful in the theology that has developed over the past several decades. Perhaps the greatest weakness lies in its tendency to encourage a distorted Christian anthropology rather than a good self-image of the Christian.

The mythological figure has some foundation in Scripture, depending upon the meaning of mythological. The force of this model in Christian tradition has shown itself only recently. It can help some people to believe, since it can eliminate certain troublesome aspects of the gospel, e.g., miracles and a literal interpretation of the divinity of Jesus, as it encourages believers to ignore certain academic theological issues in favor of getting on with the task of fulfilling a concrete mission in the world. For most Christians, however, it is totally foreign to their experience, as evidenced in the sharp reaction to the proposals advanced by the English scholars in *The Myth of God Incarnate*. The theological fruitfulness is evident, if not always welcome, since it has generated much discussion and has opened new frontiers. Believers need not look upon the New Testament as absolute. Its ability to foster a sense of Christian anthropology, however, is impaired by the tendency to reduce the value of the spiritual and make the divine appear as only another way of being human.

The ethical liberator has a firm foundation in Scripture, provided that Jesus is not viewed as an extreme revolutionary, but as one who indeed challenged the existing social order. This model has appeared occasionally in the history of theology—for example, in the social gospel of late nineteenth- and early twentieth-century Protestant thought, and could be seen as the basis for the social encyclicals of Roman Catholic twentieth-century thought. Most recently, it corresponds to the social-political experience in Latin America, that of the Black movement in the United States and those of the women's movement and other minorities. It certainly helps Christians in their efforts to believe, since it is concerned with the sufferings of millions and moreover impels believers to accomplish something for the sake of others. While it reflects the religious experience of suffering groups, it is often perceived as unrelated to the experience of other Christians. Its theological fruitfulness, in spite of the efforts to present it as a position firmly based in theology, has been limited, impaired by its narrow purview. Its ability to develop a good anthropology is also limited, since it is based upon the experience of the oppressed in very specific areas of the world and under very specific conditions.

The human face of God has a firm foundation in Scripture as well as in Christian tradition. It fosters belief, since it is as meaningful in the twentieth century as in any other, with each age contributing its own perspectives. However, it lacks a strong incentive toward involvement in the world and can encourage pietism. If it is accepted in its fullest sense, though (as Jesus was the human face of God for others, so Christians must imitate him and be themselves the face of God today), then it does provide some sense of mission. Although such a model does not figure prominently in the experience of most Christians in theory, it often does in practice. Good Christians know instinctively that when they see and experience Jesus they see and experience God. Its theological fruitfulness can be demonstrated by the divergent opinions that it can sustain, and it surely emphasizes a good Christian anthropology: if Jesus is the human face of God, then every human being carries a similar possibility to manifest the divine and every human being has immense value.

The man for others certainly has a basis in Scripture. The model does not appear frequently in the history of theology, but it has achieved prominence in recent times. It encourages people to believe precisely because it impels the faithful to fulfill their Christian mission. It is not the primary experience of most Christians, but many people would like it to shape their experience of Jesus; they would be happy if they could reach out and be of service to others. Its theological fruitfulness is limited, since it does not have a broad enough base; its understanding of a strong anthropology is evident, since it concentrates on the meaning of the humanity of Jesus for others, which will enhance every person's humanity.

Finally, the model of Jesus as personal savior has a good foundation in Scripture; it has existed throughout Christian history in both orthodox and unorthodox forms. It helps some people to believe even as it hinders others. It can discourage social involvement, since it tends to be individualistic. It surely is not the experience of the majority of believers. Its theological fruitfulness is very limited, since it often is not concerned with matters of speculative theology, and while it can develop a good self-understanding for some, it can also contribute to a sense of self-depreciation in the sight of God for others.

Over the centuries members of the Church have been drawn to various models. The same will be true today. Many Church leaders and the more traditionally oriented Christian will tend toward the model of Jesus

as the Second Person of the Blessed Trinity. It is firmly
rooted in Church tradition and in their personal history.
Those involved in the social mission will probably
choose the model of ethical liberator or the man for
others; the charismatic will choose the model of personal savior; the skeptical believer will be more at ease
with the mythological figure; the speculative theologian
will prefer the human face of God.

Often these various groups will react strongly against
certain models. The official Church type may completely reject the mythological figure and feel insecure
about the ethical liberator or the man for others. The
social mission group may dismiss the Second Person of
the Blessed Trinity as being totally irrelevant, lacking
any meaning today. The charismatic may avoid the
theological models and may also react against the skepticism that might be associated with the mythological
Christ.

Can we conclude *"Chacun à son goût"*—"To each
his own"? I do not find such a position acceptable. At
the very least, there has to be cross-fertilization. No one
should think that his or her particular model has all of
the answers or that he or she cannot learn from others.
A good, healthy skepticism can help Christians, even
when generated by those who see Jesus as mythological,
and the enthusiastic acceptance of Jesus as personal
savior might do a world of good for the speculative
theologian as well as for Church bureaucrats.

The working hypothesis throughout this present study
has been that each model has its value; each has some
insight into the meaning of Jesus as experienced and
pondered on through two millennia of Christianity. The
model of Jesus as the Second Person of the Blessed
Trinity has as its great contribution the stress on the divinity of Jesus; the mythological figure guards us
against falling into a false absolutism or a false super-
naturalism; the ethical liberator and the man for others
center more upon the mission of the Church, especially

with regard to suffering minorities; the human face of God emphasizes the humanity as the expression of the divinity; the personal savior concentrates on Jesus-for-me.

This does not mean, however, that we can accept all six models without qualification. They do not agree in every way, and often they emphasize one aspect to the detriment of another. More problematically, they suggest different priorities that will profoundly affect the movement of Christianity in the century to come. If some are taken as absolutes, they could have a disastrous effect on Christianity within a generation.

The model of Jesus as Second Person of the Blessed Trinity tends to develop an ecclesiastical sterility with little relationship to people's lives. It can be rigid and conformist, since often those who maintain such a model have authority in the Church. It can stifle free thought and create an inferiority complex for anyone who tries to develop a spiritual life, since the divine Jesus is too strong a model for sinful human beings.

The ethical liberator can involve the Church in revolution and the support of violence in the name of Jesus. It can also foster the illusion that the gospel cannot be preached as long as the economically and socially deprived continue to exist.

The human face of God can so emphasize the humanity of Jesus that all sense of the divine is forgotten. It can also undermine the sense of structure in theology by assuming that we need only a basic theology of serving others, and it can encourage subjectivism.

The man for others, like the ethical liberator, can be without much theological substance and can present Christians as a group of social workers.

Finally, the personal savior can lead to fanaticism in its search for the experience of Jesus as savior.

Once we are aware of the major contribution of each model and the major drawbacks if it is accepted exclusively, is it possible to seek a paradigm, one model that responds to more of the unanswered questions and problems than all of the others, without totally excluding them?

I do not propose, either, that the models presented here are the only possible models. There have been others in Christian history: Jesus the clown, the wise man, the teacher, the superstar, etc. These six have been chosen because in my opinion they cover most of the territory. They are major models; the others are minor. Thus no one should think that one model would be adequate for Christology for all time. We are involved with the mystery of human life and the mystery of God, and surely there can never be an adequate expression of those realities. It seems to be necessary to work with models that are, and will always remain, far removed from the reality they seek to express.

One possible method would be to harmonize the models in such a way that their differences become complementary rather than mutually exclusive. To do this demands criticizing each of the models in the light of the others. In this way we might come to an understanding of Jesus that transcends the limitations inherent in each of the models. The models can interact and allow each other to emphasize good points and counter weaknesses. A theologian may want to base his or her Christology on Jesus as the human face of God, but then include in that the model of Jesus as ethical liberator to encompass the mission aspect of the faith as actually lived. In Latin America a theologian may take the ethical liberator as the fundamental model, but join to this the model of Jesus as the human face of God, while being aware of the mythological character in order to maintain a healthy skepticism about ideologies in the struggle to renew the face of the earth.

For me, the model of Jesus as the human face of God offers the greatest possibilities. It can include in it the sense of social mission as well as what-Jesus-means-for-me; it maintains the divinity without the limitations often associated with the model of Jesus as the Second Person of the Blessed Trinity. More than any other model, it can help foster a good sense of personal worth, which every individual needs, whether or not he or she is socially, economically or politically oppressed.

Of the six models, the weakest seems to be that of the Second Person of the Blessed Trinity. For centuries it has been the predominant paradigm, but in the light of developments that have taken place in recent years it seems ill-suited for the demands that are being made upon Christianity today.

I would not suggest that a person try to harmonize all the models nor homogenize them. Each model must be seen against its own background. We are involved with the age-old mystery of the relationship between God and his people, and that will always cause us to pause before we try to solve all the problems and questions. The helpful will be preserved; what is not helpful can be easily discarded. What is of God will last: what is not will fade (Acts 5:35–39).

Upon the completion of this study I would like to engage in a little prophetic activity. Certain aspects of Christology that have emerged in the recent past will in all probability continue:

1. Christology will be more and more related to the Trinity: Jesus came not to reveal himself but to reveal the Father through the power of the Spirit. The understanding of Jesus as the one who is the human face of God, just as the Word has been traditionally understood as the expression of God, will continue with a greater sense of the trinitarian understanding of our faith. It will not, however, be Augustine's study of the Trinity nor that of the Scholastics, but an attempt to relate the revelation of God in a human being, Jesus of Nazareth, to the experience of all people. This will include them in the mystery of God that is characterized by commu-

nity. Christology will not encourage isolation, but solidarity with God understood and loved as Father.

2. The impact of the liberal and often radical economic and social movement will continue to influence Christology. Since Jesus lived for others and had a special predilection for the downtrodden, all the oppressed peoples of the world, those socially or economically or politically or sexually oppressed, will have their special claim on Jesus. Their struggles for equality and freedom will profoundly influence our understanding of Jesus.

3. The need for believing that each of us is good and can experience salvation in Jesus through an enthusiastic movement or in some other personal way will continue. The meaning for the individual that Jesus offers has great importance for the continuance of Christianity.

4. The fact of pluralism in Christology, with new approaches, will contribute to a continuing development in the understanding of Jesus of Nazareth. We will never reach the time when we can say that we have discovered the eschatological, never-to-be-changed paradigm. We will always be pilgrim people in theology as well as in faith.

These predictions seem to be warranted both by the current ferment in Christology as well as by the current awareness of the social dimensions of Christianity. If the Church is to carry on its function in the world, it has to be aware of the movements that will affect the understanding of Jesus and must allow for the fulfillment of all of the potential that lies within the human spirit.

Very often the Church carries so much history on its back that only reluctantly does it move on and cast off the dust of centuries, especially when it is a question of facing the meaning of Jesus—but only if the Church shakes off that dust can new life be communicated to old forms. What the Church will be depends to a great extent on its understanding of Jesus. If that understanding is open and encouraging and speaks to the needs of millions who are searching for someone in whom they can place their faith, then the mission of the Church will continue. People will listen and hear the revelation that God has made in Jesus.

This work began as a journey that did not know its final point. Now that the last page is reached, I am more aware that the journey in understanding Jesus of Nazareth will never end. In the history of Christianity we have only attained way stations along the road. Those stopping places, however, are not without value, since they have been blessed by the labor of believers who nobly continued to seek a response to that haunting question of Jesus himself: "Who do you say that I am?"

INDEX

Adoptionism, 182

Alexandria school of theologians, 111

Agricultural symbols, urban society and, 27

Alienation, resolution of, 123

Anger of Jesus, 49

Answers to prayer, 167

Antioch school of theologians, 111

Apostles
evangelists, see Gospels
political aspirations, 91, 96

Aquinas, Thomas, 145
incarnation, 47
instrumental causality concept, 54
knowledge acquired by Jesus, 56–57

Art, images of Christ reflected in, 24, 25

"As Kingfishers Catch Fire" (quoted), 131

Atonement, Bultmann's view, 73–74

Authoritarianism and king model of Jesus, 35

Awareness of God, baptism in the spirit and, 166

Baptism in the Spirit, 166

Barth, Karl, 28, 58

Bauer, Bruno, 70, 83

Becoming, concept applied to God, 113

Behavior, image of Church affecting, 16, 20

Believer, choice of image as revealing, 25

Bible studies, Roman Catholic attitude, 15

Biblical Christology, 154–56, 177–94
Gospels
John, 70, 190–92
Luke, 52, 185–87
Mark, 70, 183–85
Matthew, 52, 188–89
salvation message, 163

Black theology, 99, 102, 103

Boethius, 44

Bonhoeffer, Dietrich, 28, 139, 140–53, 155
Christology described by, 142–43

Born-again Christianity, see Personal Savior model of Jesus

Bultmann, Rudolf, 71–81, 83

Camara, Archbishop Helder, 160

Camus, Albert, 143

Can We Trust the New Testament?, 139

Catechetics, symbols and, 29

Chalcedon, Council of, 20, 41, 42–46, 57

definitions (text), 43
significance, 44
Charismatic movement, *see*
Personal Savior model
of Jesus
Chartres, Cathedral of, 24
Childhood of Jesus
infancy, 183, 186, 187,
188
powers during, 54
Christ-event
Bultmann on, 74, 76
Jesus and, 82
Christology
divergent views in
Church, 16
images in, 25, 30–31
of liberation theologians,
88
present state of, 15–39
questions in, 147, 150
Church
Bonhoeffer's view of, 141,
146, 147, 151
as community, 141
Jesus in, 151–52, 188
models of, 20, 197
as mystical communion,
19
role of, 156–57
structure, 103
Colson, Charles, 160, 166
Commitment to Lord as savior, necessity of,
164–65, 170–71
Communion, Church as
mystical, 19
Community
charismatic movement
view of, 168–69, 171
Church as, 141
Congregation for the De-
fense of the Faith
anxiety over modern re-
search, 16–17, 42
Council of Chalcedon
and, 42

Consciousness of Jesus,
115–16
Constantinople III,
Council of, 55
human/divine, 55
Constantinople, Third
Council of (680–81),
44
Cooke, Terence Cardinal,
160
Concilium Latronum, 43
Councils
Chalcedon (451), *see*
Chalcedon, Council of
Constantinople III
(680–81), 44
Concilium Latronum, 43
Ephesus (449), 42
Thieves, Council of, 43
Vatican II, 16
Cousins, E., 31
Creation, meaning of, 122,
144
Creatureliness, 116
Creeds
Roman, 51
Nicene, 51
Criticism, biblical, 68
Bultmann, 71–83
form criticism, 72
mythological model and,
68–83
Crucifixion, 125–26
Bonhoeffer's view, 151
Mark's gospel, 183, 184

Dante (Alighieri), 38
Death
attitudes toward, 125
kingdom of God and, 90
Death of Jesus, 124–25
Mark's gospel, 183, 184
resurrection and, 126
*Declaration on the Truth of
the Gospels*, 15
Demons, 73

Demythologizing
definition, 74, 76
moral value of myth,
Bultmann on, 74
Dependency
human relationships, in,
116
Jesus on Father, 117,
129–30
suffering and, 125
Dibelius, M., 72
Dignity of man, source of,
114
Disciples, 91, 96 (See also
Apostles)
Diversity of opinion in
Church, 16
Divinity as concept, 112–13
Divinity of Jesus, 41–63
belief in, necessity of, 53
Bultmann's view of, 73
Christology and, 16
Council of Chalcedon for-
mulation, 42–46
denial of, 68
gospel emphasis, 189, 190
humanity balanced with,
111, 140
resurrection and, 127
will, as to, 44
Divino Afflante Spiritu, 15
Docetism, 51
Dogma, necessity of, 150
Door as image of Jesus, 25
Dulles, Avery, 19, 30

Ecumenism
charismatic movement
and, 168, 173, 174
Trinitarian model as hin-
dering, 62–63
Elitism, 173
Enthusiasm, 161–62
Ephesus, Council of, 42
Ethics and the Man for
Others model, 153
Evangelical movement, see
Personal Savior model
of Jesus
Evil, 105, 117–18, 175, 186
Bonhoeffer's concept of,
140–41
power of broken by Jesus,
164, 170
Evolution of humanity, 28
Exaltation, 151
Existence, Jesus as bound-
ary of, 144, 148
Existentialism, 72, 78
Exodus, 89–90
Exorcism, 73

Face of God, Human, see
Human Face of God,
Jesus as
Faith
images and, 26
theology and, 113
Fatherhood of God, 116–17
Fig tree, cursing of, 49
Forgiveness, 172
Form criticism, 72
Francis of Assisi, 152, 162
Fraud, Christianity based
on, 67, 83
Freedom, 89, 123–24
Exodus and, 89–90
Jesus' view of, 90–91
salvation as, 122, 123
Future life, 135

Gandhi, Mohandas, 135
Gate as image of Jesus, 25
Gentiles, 187
Glossolalia, 161
Gnosticism, 51
redeemer myth in, 77
Goodness, perceiving in one-
self, 117
Gospels
apocryphal, 54
apologetic, 189
credibility, 70
John, 70, 190–92

Luke, 52, 185–87
Man for Others model and, 153, 154–56
Mark, 70, 183–85
Matthew, 52, 188–89
as salvation message, 163
virgin birth treatment in, 52
Goulder, Michael, 78
Graham, Billy, 165
Guevara, "Che", 102, 104
Gunkel, H., 72

Haines, Ralph, 160
Harnack, Adolf, 145
Healing
charismatic movement, 167–68, 170
emotional, 168
failure to receive, 174
physical, 167
reconciliation as, 141, 148
Heidegger, Martin, 72
Hellenism, 72, 75, 80, 81
Herald, Church as, 19
Hermeneutics, 99
Historical Jesus
Bonhoeffer's view, 145, 148–49
denial of existence, 67, 69, 77
insignificance, 67–68
liberation theology and, 88, 90, 93–96
mythologizing of, 67–84
History, 50
Church as, 149
Jesus in gospel period, see Historical Jesus
models developed by experiencing, 33
Homosexuality, 103
Honest to God, 67, 139
Honest to God Debate, The, 139
Hopkins, Gerard Manley (quoted), 131

Hughes, Harold, 160
Hulsbosch, A., 130
Human Face of God, Jesus as, 28, 111–36
advantages, 131–34
contemporary theologians and, 130
definition, 129
disadvantages, 134–36, 203
evaluation, 200–3
evil, reaction to, 117–18
meaning of life and, 119
pastoral implications, 134
popularization, 111
resurrection and, 126
revelation and, 112
transcendence, 121
Humanity
distinguishing characteristics, 112–13
as image of God, 114
meaning of, 153
potential, 115
Humanity of Jesus
anger, 49
Chalcedon formulation, 42, 57
dignity of man and, 114
divinity balanced with, 53
eschatological aspects, 130
freedom of, 119
ordinary aspects of, 120–22
overemphasis, 140
perfection, 48–49
relationship with Father, 116
revelation and, 112, 144
self-awareness, 115–17
sexuality, 51
sin and, 49–50
uniqueness, 114
will and, 44
worship of, 48
Human life, divine value of, 132

Humiliation, 151
Hunger, 90
Hypostatic union, 42–43, 48

Ignatius of Loyola, 162
Images of God, humans as, 114
Images of the Church, attitude and, 16, 20
Imitation of Jesus, 62
Immortality, 135
Incarnation
    Bonhoeffer's view, 150–51
    mythological model and, 68, 79
    reasons for, 47–48
    transitus, 50
    virginal conception, 51
Incarnation of the Second Person of the Trinity model, 25, 46, 47–49, 146–47, 199, 201–2, 203
    advantages, 58–60
    Chalcedon formulation, 43
    disadvantages, 60–63, 203
Infancy narratives
    Luke, 186, 187
    Mark, 182
    Matthew, 188
Injustice, 90
Institution, Church as, 19
Intuition, supernatural, 35
Isaiah, 91

Jesus
    Chalcedon description, 21
    as Christ, 75, 82
    creation united in, 23
    divinity, *see* Divinity of Jesus
    experiencing, 22
    humanity, *see* Humanity of Jesus
    images of, implications of, 19

instrumental causality and, 54
Jewishness, 179
knowledge of God, 55
as mystery, 21–23, 178
study of, scientific methodology in, 16
Jews
    culture as source for Christianity, 70, 80
    exodus, 89
    human nature, Judaic theory of, 114
John XXIII (Pope), 18
John the Baptist, 183
John the Evangelist, *see* Gospels
John Paul II (Pope), 33, 140
Joseph, St., 191
Judaism, *see* Jews
Justice, 101

Kairos (apt time), 29
Kenosis, 50
Kerygma
    biblical criticism and, 72, 74
    Bultmann's view, 73–76
Kingdom of God
    building of, 92, 95–97, 99, 100
    eschatological view, 96–97, 98–99
    meaning, 93
    New Testament description, 90
    Old Testament, 91
    revolution and, 91
Knowledge of Jesus
    Constantinople III, 55
    human/divine, 55
    infused, 55–57
Knox, Ronald, 161–62, 173, 175
Kuhn, T., 36
Küng, Hans, 130

Lamb of God as image, 25
Latin America, liberation
    theology in, 88, 99,
    102, 103
Lazarus, 173
Legends
    birth and resurrection of
        Jesus as, 68–69
    miracles as, 69
Leo I (the Great), (Pope),
    42
Leontius, 44
Lessing, G. E., 68
Letters and Papers from Prison, 139
Liberation in New Testament, 163
Liberator model of Jesus,
    34, 87–107, 200, 202
    advantages, 102–4, 106
    disadvantages, 104–6, 203
Life
    loss as saving, 151
    meaning, *see* Meaning of
        life
    values in, 153
Light as image of Jesus, 25
Logos
    creation and, 190
    daily life as, 168–69
    evolution of concept, 182
    John's gospel, 190
Logos model of Jesus, *see*
    Incarnation of the Second Person of the Trinity model
Loneliness, resolution of,
    123
Lord as image of Jesus, 25
Love
    acceptance as law of existence, 148
    universality of God's, 122
Loyola, Ignatius, 34
Luke the Evangelist, *see*
    Gospels
Luther, Martin, 144

McBrien, Richard, 19
Man for Others model, 28,
    139–57, 201–3
    advantages, 152–54
    disadvantages, 155–57,
    203
Mark, *see* Gospels
Marxism, 98, 105
Mary
    theotokos, 43
    treatment by Jesus, 49
    virginity of, 51–52
Matthew, *see* Gospels
Maximus the Confessor, 44
Meaning of life
    charismatic movement
        view of, 169
    death and resurrection
        and, 126
    Jesus as exemplifying,
        118–20, 144, 151, 153
    suffering and, 125
Mediator, Jesus as, 148, 149
    Scotus on, 48
Memories, healing of, 168
Mercy of Jesus, 186
Messiah, 25, 69, 75, 148–49
    Matthew's gospel, 188–90
    New Testament understanding, 182
    political, 69, 91, 95–96
Methodology
    mystery as effecting, 23
    scientific, limits of, 31
Miracles
    charismatic movement,
        168, 174
    mythological interpretation, 68–69, 73
    performed by Jesus, 52
    resurrection as, 57–58
Miracle worker as image of
    Jesus, 25
Missions (parish), 165
Models of Jesus
    compatibility, 195
    criteria, 195–98

evaluation, 32–36, 195–207

functional, 152

images compared with, 30

as paradigms, 36

plurality, necessity of, 37–38

scientific models compared with, 30–31

scriptural, 32

Models of the Church, 19

Morality, liberation theology and, 104

Mother Theresa of Calcutta, 152

Mystery

methodology limited by, 23

nature of, 21–23

Mystici Corporis, 56

"Myth," concept of, 68, 69–70, 73

Myth of God Incarnate, The, 68, 78–82

Mythological model of Jesus, 67–84, 199, 202

advantages, 81–82

disadvantages, 82–83

Nature

liberation of, 149

Word of God, planned as, 149

Nature of Jesus

divinity, *see* Divinity of Jesus

humanity, *see* Humanity of Jesus

person and, 42

plurality (Chalcedon definition), 43

Newman, John Cardinal, 198

New Testament

ethics in, 188

evolution of Christology, 180–81, 191

Gospels, *see* Gospels

images of Jesus in, 24, 25

models supported by, 177–94, 196

nature of, 178–79

redemption concept in, 163

New Testament studies

Roman Catholic attitude, 15

scientific methodology, 16

Nicene Creed, 51

Nonconformist, Jesus as, 93–94

Nonviolence, 100, 105

Old Testament

ethics in, 188

prophecies, 188

redemption concept, 162

resurrection and, 128

studies, attitude toward, 15

On Consulting the Faithful in Matters of Dogma, 198

Ontological and functional approaches, 155

Opinion, freedom of, 104

Oppression

kingdom of God and, 100–2, 103

Man for Others model, 154

New Testament, 93–95, 97–98

Old Testament, 89–92, 97

Oral tradition, mythological model and, 72

Original Sin, 137 n

Pain, kingdom of God and, 90

Pantheism, 136

Parables, 92, 94

Paradigms, 36–38

Parenthood of God, Jesus and, 116–17
Parousia, 180–81
Passion of Jesus, 183, 184
Pastoral approaches, mythological model and, 81, 82
Paternity of Jesus, 50
Patrick, Saint, 29
Paul VI (Pope), 17, 140
Paul of Tarsus, 75
    Christianity, authorship of, 75
    Christology of, 179, 180
    on creation, 22
Pentecostal movement, *see* Personal Savior model of Jesus
Perception, nature of, 18
Persecution of Christians, 185
Personal Savior model of Jesus, 159–76, 201–3
    advantages, 170–73
    disadvantages, 173–75, 203
Person of Jesus
    Chalcedon definition, 43
    nature and, 42
Pharisees, 91, 95
Philo, 70
Pius XII (Pope), 15, 56
Political model of Jesus, 87–93, 95
Popes
    John XXIII, 18
    John Paul II, 33, 140
    Leo I (the Great), 42
    Paul VI, 17, 140
    Pius XII, 15, 56
Poverty, 196
Prayer, Jesus as Man of, 186–87
Prayer groups, 160, 166
Preexistence of Jesus, 16, 191

Present life, emphasis on, 152
Princesse lointaine, La, 162
Process in Kingdom of God, 92
Prophecy, 52, 188
    charismatic movement and, 161
Prophet, image of Jesus as, 25, 53
Protestantism, Trinitarian model and, 58

"Q" narrative, 72
Quietism, 23

Rahner, Karl, 21, 130, 135
    authority in the Church, 34
    evolutionary image, 28
Ramsey, I. T., 30
Reconciliation, Jesus and, 141, 148
Redemption
    minimal act necessary for 54
    New Testament, 163
    Old Testament, 163
    suffering and, 125
Reimarus, H. S., 68–69, 83
Rejection of Jesus, 184
Relationships, 152
    Church and, 141
    Jesus with Father, 126, 129
Religionless Christianity, 157–58
Religious liberty, 33
Remaking of the Church, The, 19
Resurrection, 57–58
    belief in, 126
    Bonhoeffer's view of, 151
    disciples, effect on, 127–29
    meaning of, 126, 128–29, 151

mythological model and, 75–76

Revelation of God
humanity of Jesus as, *see* Human Face of God, Jesus as
human nature as limiting, 112

Revival meetings, 165

Revolutionary view of Jesus, 91

Robinson, J.A.T., 28, 67, 139–40, 142, 155

Rock as image of Church, 27

Roman Creed, 51

Royalty of Jesus, 91, 95

Ruler as model of Jesus, 35

Rusticus the Deacon, 44

Sacrament(s)
charismatic movement and, 174
Church as, 20
Jesus as, 147

Sacrament of Encounter, 28

"Safeguarding Basic Christian Beliefs" (declaration by Congregation for the Defense of the Faith), 16–17

Saints, *see* individual names

Salvation, 130, 163–64
Christ as event of, 50
freedom and, 122, 123
as healing, 170
in liberation theology, 98
as mystery, 21

Savior model, *see* Personal Savior model of Jesus

Schillebeeckx, Edward, 28, 130, 135

Schmidt, K. L., 72

Scholarship, 174

Scholasticism, views of on incarnation, 45

on the Trinity and Jesus, 46

Schoonenberg, P., 130, 135

Science, mythological model and, 78

Scotus, Duns, 47–48

Scripture, 60, 153–55, 177–79
gospels, *see* Gospels
inerrancy, 174
studies, Church and, 15

Second coming, 181

Second Person of the Trinity model of Jesus, *see* Incarnation of the Second Person of the Trinity model

Self-understanding of Jesus, 54, 115–16

Servant image, 19, 25, 28, 155

Servant model, *see* Man for Others model of Jesus

Sexuality, 51

Shamrock symbol, 29

Shepherd image of Jesus, 25

Sin, 117–18, 120, 122, 165
original, 47–50, 72–73, 75, 122, 137 n

Slavery, 89, 90

Sobrino, Juan, 88

Social classes, 94

Social encyclicals, 200

Social justice, 156

Social order
evolution of Kingdom in, 92, 95–99, 100
human role in development, 91, 96, 97–98, 102
Jesus and, 88–90, 154

Social problems, 123, 154

Son of Abraham, 188

Son of David, 188

Son of God, Jesus as, 187, 191

Son of Man, Jesus as,

184–85, 190
Speaking in tongues, 161
Stapleton, Ruth Carter, 160
Strauss, D. F., 69, 74, 83
Suffering
  Bonhoeffer's view of, 143
  Jesus and, 124, 125,
    183–85, 189
  kingdom of God and, 90
  meaning of, 125, 126, 175
Suffering servant theme,
  125, 126
  gospel treatment, 183–85,
    189
Summa Theologica, 145
Symbols
  breakdown of, 26–27
  new, 28–29
  role of, 26–27
Systematic Theology, 139

Teacher, Jesus as, 24, 188
Terminology, changing,
  17–18
Theandric acts, 52, 55
Theodosius, Emperor, 42
Theology
  (*See also* individual
    models and topics)
  definition, 17
  evolution of, 17, 61, 83
  images in, 25
  value of, 23–24
Theresa of Calcutta,
  Mother, 152

Thomism, 46
Tillich, Paul, 79, 139
  life cycle of image, 28
Tomus ad Fulvium, 42
Tongues, speaking in, 161
Tradition, model compati-
  bility with, 197
Transcendence, human,
  130–31
Translation problems, 42,
  43–44
Trinitarian model of Jesus,
  see Incarnation of the
  Second Person of the
  Trinity model
Trinity, 16, 41–46, 51–53

Universe, early views of, 73

Vatican II, effects of, 15–16
Vincent de Paul, 152
Vine as image of Jesus, 25
Violence, 34, 95, 105
Virgin birth, 51–52

Will of Jesus, 44
Women
  in liberation theology, 103
  Luke's gospel, 187
Word, *see* Logos
World War I, effects of, 71

Young, F., 79

Zealots, 94, 95, 96

SCRIPTURAL INDEX

Genesis:
  1:27   113
Exodus:
  5:1   89
  34:20   162
Numbers:
  18:15   162

Deuteronomy:
  7:8   162
  24:18   162
Psalms:
  22:1, 3, 9, 11   184
Isaiah:
  11:6   91

41:4	191
43:10	191
46:4	191
65:17	91
66:22	91

Jeremiah:
15:10	162

Daniel:
7:13–14	181
7 and 9	69

Matthew:
1:1	188
2:11	189
4:26–29	92
5:1–7:29	188
7:20	35
9:13	94
11:3–5	90
13:24–30	92
13:27	53
13:33	92
14:33	189
16:16	189
20:28	163
25:31–46	180
26:52	189
28:17–20	190
28:18	36

Mark:
1:4	91
1:11	182
1:14	183, 185
1:27	188
2:15–17	94
2:27	93
3:18–19	94
3:21	121
8:31	183, 184
9:30	183
9:31	183, 185
10:11–12	93
10:18	49
10:33	183, 185
10:34	183

10:45	154, 163, 184
13:9–13	185
14:41	185
14:61	180

Luke:
1:32	187
2:11	186
2:30	164
2:31–32	187
2:34	93
3:21	186
3:22	187
4:18	90, 94, 186
4:18–21	90
4:21	90, 186
4:31	186
4:36–37	186
5:16	186
5:17–26	186
6:6–11	186
6:11–17	187
6:12	186
7:9	187
7:36–50	187
8:43–48	187
9:18	187
9:28–29	187
9:46	94
10:18	164
10:20	186
10:22	187
11:1	187
12:8	180
15:1	94
15:10	186
17:19	187
22:22	187
22:25–28	93
22:29	187
22:39–45	187
23:46	187
23:55	187
24:49	187

John:
1:1	173, 182

1:12	190	8:22–23	22, 90
1:13	190	8:24	164
1:18	173	8:38–39	172
1:45	191	12:2	142
2:13–15	191		
5:22	36	**1 Corinthians:**	
6:15	95	1:30	163
7:43	93	6:14	163
9:16	93	15:28	91
10:19	93		
10:35	191	**2 Corinthians:**	
14:9	113, 133, 191	4:14	163

Acts:

1:1 ff.	187	**Ephesians:**	
1:16	96	1:7	163
2:32	125	1:10	22
2:34b	125	2:1–10	164
2:36	182	3:8	22
3:12–26	180		
4:9–12	180	**Philippians:**	
5:30–32	180	3:10	163
5:35–39	205	3:20	164
13:26	163		
16:17	163	**Colossians:**	
		1:14	163

Romans:

		1:15	114, 128
1:4	178, 181	3:9	22
1:16	163		
3:24	163	**1 Timothy:**	
4:25	163	1:15	164
6:1 ff.	163		
7:19	118	**Hebrews:**	
8:14–17	164	1:3	114
		4:15	32, 114, 183
		9:15	163
		9:28	164

ABOUT THE AUTHOR

FATHER JOHN F. O'GRADY is presently a Visiting Professor of Theology at Duquesne University in Pittsburgh. Prior to this position he was Dean of Academic Affairs and Professor of New Testament Theology at St. Bernard's Seminary in Rochester, New York. The author of two previous books, *Jesus, Lord and Christ* and *Christian Anthropology*, Father O'Grady has also written many articles on Biblical Theology.

30D